HEATHER BUTLER
JIM BUTLER
PAM HENDERSON

THE **ULTIMATE**
INSIDER'S GUIDE TO
FINDING THE PERFECT

Wedding Dress

BRIDAL TRAINING
&
MARKETING SYSTEMS

This publication is designed to provide accurate and authoritative information in regard to the subject matter covered. It is sold with the understanding that the publisher is not engaged in rendering legal, accounting, or other professional service. If legal advice or other expert assistance is required, the services of a professional should be sought.

Butler, Heather R.; Butler, James K.; Henderson, Pam
    The Ultimate Insiders Guide to Finding the Perfect Wedding Dress

ISBN 978-0-578-09506-6
    1. Fashion

Printed in the United States of America

*To brides across the world as they
begin their exciting quest for the
perfect wedding dress*

CONTENTS

CONTENTS

Introduction

Pam Henderson

Hi, I'm Pam Henderson of Camarillo Bridal.

I'm so excited by your recent engagement and thank you for purchasing a copy of my book, The Ultimate Insider's Guide to Finding the Perfect Wedding Dress in Southern California. I have written this book with several top bridal retailers across the country to help you find the perfect wedding gown as you plan your wedding. I think you'll find this book will save you a lot of time and money and will be one of the best resources you'll be able to turn to again and again as you prepare for the wedding of your dreams.

I've been dressing brides in California for over 10 years. I'm excited to share with you in this introduction some things that are unique to our area that that you should carefully consider before buying your gown.

At Camarillo Bridal you will have a world-class experience dealing with our professional bridal consultants. Our experienced bridal specialists will be standing by, ready to assist you with your every need, every day. We take the guesswork out of planning everything you'll wear on one of the most important days of your life!

You will notice and appreciate the difference from the minute you step into our beautiful new store. You will be greeted warmly by our Director of First Impressions and assisted in completing a simple bridal registry form. This form will help your bridal consultant get a sense of your personal style and the ideas you've already put together for your wedding plans. Your personal bridal consultant will help you try on different gown silhouettes and assist you in finding the best one for you! Our family owned salon assures you that all your wedding needs will be given the utmost priority. Your trust in our salon will be earned from the minute you enter our lobby. You will find that once you are a Camarillo Bridal Bride, you become family!

As a Southern Californian bride, you know that you can take advantage of the beautiful year-round temperate weather and choose any season for your special day. In California you can enjoy wonderful ocean vistas, tranquil vineyards, scenic deserts, world-renowned golf courses or rustic mountain venues. Whether you are getting married in one of the many outdoor areas available to our California brides, or in your hometown church or synagogue, you'll find your choices are limitless! At Camarillo Bridal we have helped thousands of brides get married in all sorts of venues. There are some beautiful parks, gardens, beaches, winery's, mountains, churches and farms. Each venue has a special meaning and can be enjoyed by your guests. As you read all the great information in this book, you'll find ideas that will fit your venue and time of year. Please read on about how Camarillo Bridal can help you with the Wedding of Your Dreams.

You'll enjoy our incredible selection of gowns. Put simply, you won't find such an extensive collection of gowns anywhere else in Southern California. Why go to New York, Chicago or even downtown Los Angeles, when you can find your gown here at Camarillo Bridal. Some of our limited edition exclusive gowns can not be found anywhere else in California. You'll delight in our cutting edge gowns, made just for our salon by outstanding designers, that we work with personally to bring in the best looks. Why wear a "cookie cutter" gown that is found all over the internet and at those big box stores, when you can have an outstanding gown that is found exclusively at Camarillo Bridal. The chapter on Why buying a Dress Online won't save you money is a real eye opener. Our gowns showcase your unique style and personality in such a stunning way that every eye will be on you throughout your big day! Shopping at Camarillo Bridal is the same as going to 8-10 other smaller stores who just don't have the extensive inventory that we do. Make sure you ready the chapters on The History of the Gown, Silhouettes, Shapes and Styles as well as The 10 Commandments of Shopping for your Dress. These chapters will help you when you are ready for your appointment here. At Camarillo Bridal we bring all 4 silhouettes to you in hundreds of choices just for you.

Our 5-point Premium Care Treatment begins with the inspection of the gown. Looking over all the lace, beadwork and appliques. Making sure it's exactly as ordered. Then we trim all loose threads, make sure the buttons, hook and eyes and zippers are in impeccable condition. Third we give the gown a pressing/steaming. Many stores do not steam or press the gown when it arrives. We provide a breathable, cloth bag along with a sturdy hanger that will protect your gown in the best possible way in preparation for your wedding. Camarillo Bridal also give you the option of a 2nd pressing after your alterations are done, so that you won't worry about looking wrinkled as you walk down the aisle. No other store in Southern California provides this 5-point Premium care Treatment like we do.

Camarillo Bridal is one of the most highly recommended locally owned bridal salons in Southern California. For over 12 years, thousands of brides have entrusted their wedding experiences to our store and staff, in addition, over 70% of the brides who buy from us have been referred by one of their friends who have also had a great experience at our store. With so many brides, their families and friends working with us you know you're in great hands. Our customer service goes beyond mere words. We promise to do our utmost in helping you with all of your bridal attire needs. We'll handle the details for you! And this book will go a long way in helping you navigate this most exciting time in your life.

You'll receive exclusive membership in our Preferred Buyers Program available ONLY to our customers that will allow you to save BIG money on jewelry, tuxedos, bridesmaids, mothers and other wedding attire and accessories. With our Platinum or Gold membership you'll save money when you purchase your gown on your first visit. Your Bridal Specialist will be able to explain how she can save you money on your first appointment with her. Speaking of your first appointment.... At Camarillo Bridal we give each of our brides a FREE gift just for coming in!

Our unique and stylish bridesmaid dresses are available in over 55 colors, even your pickiest bridesmaid will LOVE! Our Bridal Consultants will love to assist you with finding the perfect bridesmaid gown to compliment your wedding ensemble. Make sure you read the chapter on Dressing the Bridesmaids, you'll gain lots of tips and ideas to help make this one of the most pleasurable experiences in your wedding shopping! In fact, this little book will become indispensable to you as you go shopping for all your wedding needs.

You won't want to miss the information shared in the chapters for dressing the Groom and the Men's fashion tips. Including the groom in your planning will keep him in the know. The men in your wedding party will play a special role and you'll want them dressed to the nines! Camarillo Bridal works with one of the bet in the business, Jim's Formal Wear. Jim's is another family owned business, where they never forget the importance of your special day. Our bridal specialists will help you coordinate the tuxedos with the rest of your bridal party, you'll love the finished look. And not to forget the mothers in the wedding! Camarillo Bridal has one of the largest selection, bar none, of Mother's dresses in California! We keep our stock fresh and updated. I personally pick out every style as if I was wearing it myself. Gone is the day of the frumpy Mother of the Bride. You and your groom's mom is guaranteed to look appropriately stunning after shopping our collection of unique and beautiful Mother of the bride or groom dresses. We also have shoes, jewelry and undergarments to complete their look.

And speaking of Undergarments.... Don't forget to read chapter 15 (my personal favorite) about the proper foundations that will turn your gown from great to SPECTACULAR. At Camarillo Bridal, our bridal consultants are also specialists in fitting the proper undergarments. We have a large selection of bustiers that would even make Victoria blush... We do a VERY GOOD JOB at fitting large and hard to fit busts. We are proud to support California-made products and our petticoat company sews your petticoat a mere 50 miles from here.

Come "shop" our vendor library and find great deals from local wedding vendors that will make your wedding planning even easier!

Over the years our brides tell us they're surprised at how easy it is to afford our unparalleled world-class quality gowns. Camarillo Bridal makes the process of getting your wedding gown easy, stress-free, without any of the high pressure you might experience at other salons. But you don't have to take their word for it, find out for yourself! We're confident you'll say the same and know you'll be delighted when you visit Camarillo Bridal!

CHAPTER 1

HISTORY OF THE GOWN (FROM QUEEN VICTORIA TO YOU)

RHONDA SHEMWELL-SHELTON

Congratulations on your upcoming wedding. Being a bride is so exciting! One of the most fabulous parts about being a bride is choosing your wedding gown. Choosing "THE" gown should be a relaxing experience with a knowledgeable, trained consultant at YOUR side assisting YOU with YOUR wedding vision. Please note the capitalized words in the previous sentence. The bridal choice is the decision of the Bride with *input* from only her most trusted relatives and friends.

We have had brides come into our stores and ask us why most bridal gowns are white or a version of white. Why do wedding gowns have a train? Can I wear another color? The goal of the next few pages is to answer a few of these same questions and assist you in choosing your dream gown.

Brides throughout the centuries have always worn their best attire for the wedding. All participants of the wedding, including guests, donned the best clothing they had, or the best they could afford, for the ceremony and the following celebration. It wasn't until the wedding of Queen Victoria to Albert of Saxe in 1840 that a white wedding gown became the "in" thing to wear. Most people believe white was chosen because it signifies purity, but that is not the case. Prior to and during the 1800s, the color blue was considered to be the color of purity and white signified and represented wealth. So, in turn, white became the color of choice for the wealthy and elite.

Queen Victoria's wedding was a very opulent event. To further the social impact of her day, she not only selected white for her bridal gown color but the dress makers added a train to her gown. The significance of the train was to further exemplify the show of great wealth. Fabric, at this time, was not an easy commodity to come by. It was hand loomed and manufactured very slowly. To have a lot of fabric in any garment was a definitive way to demonstrate your wealth and status. As time moved on and the advent of the Industrial Revolution occurred, fabric could be made by machines. Consequently, the cost of fabric significantly dropped. With a much more plentiful fabric supply, the marketplace was being opened for clothing to be more available and much more affordable. The bridal gown was no exception to the laws of supply, demand, and price. Brides were more able to wear a gown that was made and designed specifically for them for the wedding day.

Around the turn of the century, white bas the premium color choice for a bride. However, the styles were continually evolving because of changes in economies, current events, and trends. One of the best examples of this is the "Roaring 20s" flapper era. Brides of this time adopted a modified flapper gown of a shortened hemline as opposed to a long, floor length type of gown. Even though the hemline came up, a train was still present on the shorter length gowns but its form had changed to that of a Watteau train (see chapter on Bridal Silhouettes). The grandeur and glamour of the 20s took to a staggering halt with the onset of the Great Depression.

When the Great Depression hit, followed by the start of World War II, bridal fashions took another turn. Brides continued to want a white gown, but in many cases, a white gown was impractical due to its cost and usability. Times were hard and money had to be spent for necessities. Those that could afford to purchase or make their white gown would many times choose to dye it 1ZA478T50342410042 a more practical color after the wedding. At this time many pastel colors came into vogue for their practicality. Brides that felt compelled to dye their white gowns to a more practical color would save the collar or cuffs as their keepsake memento for the day. As the Great Depression started to wind down, the United States was faced with an even bigger threat of war with Germany and Japan.

During World War II many weddings were held quickly with little notice. War Brides (as they were known), usually had little time to prepare because the fiancé would be deployed very quickly. Unfortunately, War Brides were destined to wear a suit or their best dress for the occasion. During this time the advent of the "ready wear" bridal store began to take shape. Instead of purely custom made gowns by dressmakers, women now had a choice of gowns that were "on the rack" and could be bought immediately and taken out of the store. When World War II was finally over manufacturing went from "war" goods to "soft" goods. Fabrics became more plentiful and the economy became much stronger. Because brides had fabrics and time on their side to actually plan and prepare for the wedding, they were back to purchasing and custom designing their bridal attire.

In the 1950s the wedding of Grace Kelly to Prince Rainier in Monaco set the stage for the present day bride. Her gown consisted of a voluminous skirt, hand made laces, seed pearls, and a train of great length. Her gown was the perfect choice for a future princess. Princess Grace's gown, created by an MGM costume designer, is still very influential in today's bridal fashions. While Princess Grace was the epitome of bridal fashion in the early 50s; other Hollywood starlets also influenced fashions of the time.

The mid-late 1950s saw the emergence of a very new bridal gown trend that has been revived for today's brides and is growing in popularity. It was then that the tea length gown, or "Ballerina Style", came upon the scene. This type of gown was introduced by the well known dress company and designer William Cahill. Cahill's gowns were frothy and frilly. They were greatly inspired by the ballerina paintings of Degas. The gowns of Cahill featured a full tulle skirt and the bodice was usually of lace or satin or a combination of both. Lace has always been integral to the bridal gown as ornamentation. This is most evident of the gowns in the 40s and 50s.

Now that World War II was over, factories in France and Belgium returned to lace making production. World renown for the beauty and quality of their laces, the factories of both countries started production as fast and furious as they could output. Consumers were more than ready for lace goods to hit the marketplace. The laced, frilly wedding gown became a hit with postwar brides.

A combination of lace being more plentiful and Hollywood's monumental films such as "Father of the Bride," starring the iconic Elizabeth Taylor, Hollywood was (and still is) a considerable influence on what brides want to wear. When the early 1960s rolled around, glamour was still a big part of the formal wear industry. When John F. Kennedy was elected as president, First Lady Jacqueline Kennedy would be the fashion plate of the Era and the one person all the world wanted to emulate. Mrs. Kennedy introduced the sleeveless, strapless silhouette of a sheath design. The media literally pounced on the First Lady's choice and deemed it as a fashion must, for any occasion.

However, the bridal industry did not immediately adopt the sleeveless fashion. Weddings were usually held in churches and being somewhat bare was not readily accepted for many of the churches, cathedrals, or synagogues. So many modifications to the style were being made with small cap sleeves or a sheer caplet. The biggest contribution of the sixties was in 1964 when the A-line silhouette hit design houses and the "ready to wear" market place. Previously all that had been seen in the realm of bridal fashion was the Ball gown, Sheath, or Ballerina gown. Now the A-line style was introduced to the fashion scene and changed bridal design forever. Also, the sixties decade would further influence the bridal market, but not by design inspiration but more from social perspectives and influences.

In the late sixties, a trend shift to a more relaxed atmosphere with the surge of the hippie movement influenced not only the social climate but clothing trends as well. Bridals gowns were equally influenced by the political shifts of the time. Gowns became more unconstructed and were generally flowy in nature. A caftan and mideastern flavor started to be seen in the bridal industry. But not every bride wanted to go with the new look and many brides continued with some traditional bridal looks. The use of lace was still very prevalent, but the Empire and A-line silhouettes took center stage. Again Watteau trains entered back into fashion because this type of train is very conducive to the aforementioned styles. This styling continued into the early seventies.

By the middle to the end of the seventies, it was becoming evident that fashion designers were becoming very influential in the bridal industry. Consumers wanted garments with a name stamped on the label. Many young designers began their careers at this time and many made a name for themselves with fashion magazines and media hype. Even though a named label was sewn into these gowns, basic gown structures remained the same until 1980.

In 1980 the most trendsetting wedding for the next three decades happened: Lady Diana Spencer married Prince Charles. Televised for the entire world to see, Lady Diana's and Prince Charles's wedding brought back into style, the forever popular ball gown. And not just any kind of ball gown, but one that was voluminous with a train that would make even Queen Victoria jealous. Princess Diana's gown brought to the bridal industry the huge and over the top "leg o'mutton" sleeve, multiple layers of petticoats and spectacular beading.

The bridal industry went wild. Extravagant and embellished gowns, gloves, and other accessories were the predominant purchases for the 80s bride. Bridal gowns were exaggerated with tremendous amounts of bead detail, laces, appliqués and full cathedral trains.   Toward the end of the eighties, the bridal gown industry started to scale down styles and the gowns evolved into simpler and more refined versions of their previous styles.

A simpler gown with less detail continued into the nineties. The 21st century appears to be whatever the bride feels the most beautiful in wearing.   Today's bride is everywhere on the spectrum. From vintage and sleek to modern and simple designs, to over the top princess creations the bridal industry is literally, "seeing it all". The sky is the limit for today's bride. It is a matter of individual taste, style, and budget.

The bridal gown has evolved throughout the decades for so many reasons. Whether it has changed for social standards, style, designers or celebrity trends, brides throughout history have wanted nothing more than to be beautiful on a very special and rare day of their life. So, regardless of color, style or expense, the bridal gown is the most important purchase a person makes for their wedding. Brides should always remember that when selecting their gown they should choose what they really love. Twenty, thirty, fifty years from the wedding, the memory that will be forever engrained in your groom's mind will be how beautiful you were in your gown. The guests, the food, the flowers will all fade from the mind, but the gown..... Never.

CHAPTER 2

SILHOUETTES, SHAPES, AND STYLES: HOW TO KNOW WHICH DRESS WILL FIT YOU BEST

HEATHER AND JIM BUTLER

The search for your wedding gown can be an overwhelming experience if you're not sure what to look for. Your choice will be much easier when you know the four silhouettes of wedding gowns and which one will look most flattering on your figure. Wearing the right cut of gown for your body type can draw attention to your best features and minimize those you're concerned about.

The four silhouettes (ball gown, empire, princess cut and sheath) all create varying visual effects on different body types. If you haven't tried on wedding dresses before, it is recommended that you try on at least one dress in each silhouette. This will allow you to see which cut best complements the look and feel you are trying to evoke at your wedding.

The Ball Gown

The ball gown has a form-fitting bodice with a full skirt. It is the most traditional of all wedding gowns. Ball gowns can have several types of waistlines. These include:

- **Basque** features a fitted bodice with an elongated triangle beneath the front and center of the waistline. This style diminishes the width of the dress at the waist.

- **Natural** waistline for this dress is between the hip and the ribcage

- **Asymmetrical** features a change in waist height from one side of the dress to the other

- **Dropped** falls several inches below the natural waistline. This style of dress elongates the torso.

The Sheath

The sheath is a form fitting dress that closely follows the line of the body. The skirt has either a slit in the front, side or back of the dress or can flare out into a trumpet or fishtail style to make walking easier.

The Princess Cut or A-Line

Princess cut or A-line gowns have an A-shape, created by vertical seams
running from the shoulders to a flared skirt, and are characterized by
their narrow-at-the-top, wider at the bottom shape. This style of gown is
designed to elongate the lines of the body by adding a classic elegance and
an illusion of length. This dress doesn't have a defined waistline. It fits
through the torso and then flares out from the waist.

The Empire

The empire has a high waisted seam just below the bustline that falls into a sheath or A-line skirt. The skirt begins two or more inches above the natural waistline and has a slender fit. This waist-minimizing cut allows extra room for brides who have tummy concerns or are pregnant.

The chart that follows has several suggestions for consideration when trying on these silhouettes based on your body type. Remember these are generalized recommendations, and you will still want to try on the different styles to find out what fits you best and what you feel prettiest in. Body shapes can vary tremendously and there is no one size fits all approach. Talk with your bridal consultant about which fit is best for you.

Figure Type	Things to Consider	Things to Avoid
Hour Glass Figure (small waist, full hips and bust)	Princess cut gown with a v-neck or scoop-neck is flattering.	Empire silhouette may hide your figure or make it look disproportional.
Short Waisted and Petite	Princess cut elongates a short waist and lengthens the torso.	A sheath will make your short waist more obvious.
Long Waist	A basque waist ball gown will give you the appearance of a shorter waistline.	A princess cut will elongate you and make your long waist more obvious.
Boxy (undefined waistline-the line from your shoulders to your hips is straight)	An empire-waist gown will de-emphasize your waistline and give you a long, thinning look. Horizontal detailing will draw the eye across the body and combat vertical body lines, and oversized shoulders and sleeves will add width to your top and shape to your overall appearance.	A princess cut or sheath will draw too much attention to your middle.
Pear-Shaped (smaller on top, heavier on the bottom)	Choose a gown that will draw attention to the upper half of your body. The silhouette isn't quite as important as the neckline you select. An off the shoulder neckline will flatter your shoulders and chest while drawing focus away from your hips.	A sheath will be unflattering. The neckline is important here – but avoid a V-neck that draws the eyes down.
Full Figure / Plus Size	The ball gown is full and will hide many figure problems in the lower areas. Minimize a thick waist with an empire waistline. A princess cut will flatter practically any figure.	A sheath will make you look heavier than you are.

CHAPTER 3

THE 10 COMMANDMENTS OF SHOPPING FOR YOUR DRESS: WHAT YOU MUST KNOW AND DO BEFORE BUYING YOUR WEDDING DRESS

HEATHER AND JIM BUTLER

The quest for your wedding gown can be one of the most exciting and fun-filled parts of planning for your wedding. Your gown will set the tone for your entire wedding and there are few other times where you will be so lavishly pampered as you are magically transformed into a beautiful bride before your very eyes. But before you buy your wedding gown, here are ten things that you need to know and do:

1. Get a clear picture of what you want your wedding to look like in your mind.
Close your eyes and envision yourself as a bride. What do you see?

Are you going to be walking down an aisle, getting married outside or uttering your vows by the soft glow of candlelight? Will you be wearing a full ball gown with your hair up and a long flowing veil? Or are you dressed in a flowing, romantic gown that accentuates your femininity? Write down six adjectives that best describe how you want to look and feel on your wedding day. For example, you may write words such as: traditional, romantic, princess like, lavish, minimalist, sexy, sophisticated, etc.

2. Try on the different silhouettes of gowns to find out what looks best on your figure.

All wedding gowns fall under four basic silhouettes: the ball gown (the most traditional of the categories, has a full bodice and waistline that leads to a very full skirt), the empire (has a high waistline which falls to a slimmer skirt), the A-line or princess (features vertical seams flowing from the shoulders down to an A-shaped flared skirt) and the sheath (closely follows the line of the body). An experienced bridal consultant can point out the features of how you look in each. You should let her know what you like about each style as well.

3. Select the color and fabric of your gown.

The same dress style can look and feel quite different in a different color or fabric. Even though white has traditionally been the color of most gowns, more and more gowns are being designed with color in the details. You may want to consider an off white, ivory or blush/champagne color as a way to enhance your complexion. Choose a color and fabric that best reflects the mood you are trying to create at your wedding. When choosing the fabric, keep in mind that it will be the basis for the overall look and feel of your gown and will influence cost more than any other single thing. Textured material and overlays such as chiffon, tulle, and organza can also be used to create a special look for you.

4. Determine what features you want on your gown.

These features include the type of neckline, waistline, train, beadwork or lace on the bodice and skirt, and other decorations or embellishments.

Once you have determined which silhouette, color and fabric you like best, determine if the gown will have sleeves, straps or if you prefer strapless. You will want to try on a variety of gowns to help you find what you like best as you bring "the perfect gown" into closer focus.

5. Accept help from knowledgeable and professional bridal consultants.

A good bridal consultant will ask lots of questions to get more clarity about your special day. They will want to be helpful to you and may have some recommendations for you. An expert consultant has seen gowns on many women in various shapes and sizes and will be able to recommend a dress that will look great on your body. Let an expert's opinion guide you to considering some shapes or styles you might never have imagined wearing. However, your consultant should make you feel comfortable and free to express your own opinion. From the moment you enter the salon, be mindful of the way you're being treated and of the way the salespeople make you feel. Do they treat you with respect? This is your special day and you deserve help that makes you feel comfortable and happy.

6. Be aware of traditions or religious guidelines that may influence how your gown should look.

Different pastors, clergy or officiants of weddings in various religious and/or ethnic backgrounds require that your head, legs or shoulders be covered. It is best to check with your ceremony officiant to find out if he/she has any guidelines that may need to be considered before you buy your gown. This will prevent embarrassment on the part of you and your guests.

7. Bring along someone whose opinion you trust and respect to help you in your search.

This person could be your mother, sister, bridesmaid, honor attendant, a close friend or another relative. An extra set of eyes can be helpful, but limit the number of people who come with you. Too many opinions will likely confuse you and lead to a frustrating experience. Such feedback can be invaluable. But, remember, it is your wedding, so you should make the final decision after careful consideration of your choices.

8. Make your decision.

Making your final decision doesn't have to be stressful. You have your mother or friend and your consultant to help you. Be sure to give yourself a chance to look at several options before you buy. Trust your own instincts. You have likely been visualizing this day for some time. Ask yourself these three questions of the final dresses that you are seriously considering: 1) Which dress do I feel the prettiest in?, 2) Which dress accentuates my best feature? and 3) Which dress best fits my personality or style? Try on each gown and go through this process until you have eliminated all of the dresses to the final one. Once you've found a gown that is everything you've imagined, smile and relax – you've found it!

9. Have your dress altered to match your exact figure.

Once you have your gown, find a professional seamstress, who is an expert at altering wedding gowns, to help you make the final alterations that will help your dress fit perfectly. Many bridal stores will have their own seamstress on site to help you. This process usually involves an initial fitting and one to two more alteration appointments. Following these fitting appointments, your dress will be pressed. You may want to wait until a few days before your wedding before you pick it up.

10. Look for the final touches that will help you complete your gown and make your wedding day special.

Once you've found your gown, look for matching elements such as a veil, shoes, and gloves that will make your transformation into a new bride complete. You may want to ask your bridal consultant for suggestions for these final touches.

With these ten tips in mind, your quest for your wedding gown should now be an exciting, fulfilling and wonderful experience. Have fun!

CHAPTER 4

TOP 10 MOST SHOCKING AND OUTRAGEOUS WEDDING DRESS MYTHS

HEATHER AND JIM BUTLER

As a recently engaged bride, you have likely been exposed to a lot of information that will help you plan the perfect wedding. There are many myths and superstitions surrounding weddings which have been passed down from generation to generation. Many of the things you hear today simply aren't true or are just downright hilarious. In fact, many wedding traditions followed today are the result of superstitions created by myth and folklore (particularly surrounding avoiding bad luck and evil spirits) and the original meaning has been lost or forgotten over the years.

So, how do you sort through the voluminous amounts of myth and folklore and pick what will define your wedding as one you will always remember and one that all of your friends and relatives will envy for years to come? Everyone has an opinion, but how will you know what is just right for you?

Over the years, we've heard many different myths that brides have believed and have been relieved to find out that they weren't true or that they didn't need to worry about them. From all of the things we've heard over the years personally from brides we've worked with or from the bridal consultants in our store, we've put together a list of the top ten most shocking and outrageous wedding dress myths to help you sort through the misinformation and find out what will help you plan your wedding without stress, confusion or worry.

Many myths you'll hear conflict with one another and have different meanings depending on how they have been used to foretell good and bad luck. Even though most myths brides hear aren't true, it doesn't stop them from going all out to make sure they haven't missed anything and to ensure that their wedding will be great. Our goal in sharing these top ten dress myths is to help you know what they are and why they aren't true so you can say yes to your dress with confidence and excitement. Here are the top ten myths and our thoughts about them:

Myth #1 A wedding dress should be white. You shouldn't wear a white wedding gown if you're not a virgin or if it is your second or third marriage. The most popular color of wedding dresses today is ivory. The color white was traditionally chosen to imitate the color of Queen Victoria's dress when she wed Albert in 1840. While many have embraced that tradition, the reality is that prior to that time, the majority of wedding gowns were either silver or red. Today, brides can choose whatever color they wish, whether they are virgins or not, and whether it is their first marriage, second or third. The only thing that matters regarding the color of your wedding gown is that it is a color that you want to wear. Quite simply, it is your choice.

One funny poem written in the 1800s that describes a bride's fate depending on the color of dress she got married in reveals the silliness of traditions regarding color:

"Married in White, you have chosen right

Married in Grey, you will go far away,

Married in Black, you will wish yourself back,

Married in Red, you will wish yourself dead,

Married in Green, ashamed to be seen,

Married in Blue, you will always be true,

Married in Pearl, you will live in a whirl,

Married in Yellow, ashamed of your fellow,

Married in Brown, you will live in the town,

Married in Pink, your spirit will sink."

Again, it is your wedding and you can choose whatever color of dress you would like to wear that you'll feel beautiful and comfortable in. That is what matters most of all.

Myth #2 I've got lot's of time as I'm not getting married for six months to a year. Following your engagement, it is easy to get caught in the trap that you've got lots of time as you plan your wedding. However, as you've probably discovered, time passes quickly and it takes time to construct and complete the intricate details that a wedding gown requires. Brides magazine recommends that you get your dress at least a year before you get married. There is so much to do as you plan your wedding and your dress will be the centerpiece of everything you do. Prices on fabric have been increasing due to the effects of inflation, so if you see a dress you love, you should get it before the price increases (because it likely will). If you need extra length because of your height, you also need to plan ahead and order your dress early. By getting that decision out of the way, you'll be able to focus on all of the other details that will go into planning your perfect dress.

Myth #3 In order to find the perfect dress, you have to look endlessly on web sites and try on lots of gowns at every store in town. It is easy to get overwhelmed when you start looking at pictures of wedding gowns. There seem to be literally thousands of styles to choose from.

As mentioned in Chapter 2, the reality is that all wedding gowns fall into one of four basic silhouettes or cuts. These are:

1. The ball gown is the most traditional of the categories and has a fitted bodice and waistline that leads to a very full skirt.

2. The empire has a high waistline (usually a line just under the bust) which falls to a slimmer skirt.

3. The princess cut features vertical seams flowing from the shoulders down to an A-shaped flared skirt.

4. The sheath closely follows the line of the body.

That's it. Just four silhouettes or styles. When you start shopping, try on one of each silhouette or style. Then, you'll be able to see how you look in each one and find out which one accentuates your best features and makes you feel absolutely beautiful and stunning (as your wedding dress should).

Myth #4 You shouldn't start shopping until you are the size you want to be on your wedding day. Another variation of this myth is that a wedding dress must fit you perfectly before you can buy it. Planning a wedding can be a very stressful experience and stress is a well-known and proven cause of weight fluctuation. In our experience, at least 98% of all of the dresses that brides buy at our store require some type of alterations. If you are planning to lose weight, it is easy and inexpensive to adjust the gown you've chosen to fit you closer to your wedding day. The problem with waiting is that you limit your choices (since gowns require time to order) and especially since a gown you love may be sold to another decisive bride. The majority of brides buy their dresses nine to eighteen months prior to their weddings with this in mind. They know they should get their alterations done closer to the date of the wedding. They plan ahead and ensure that they'll get the dress they love most and then alter it to fit perfectly right before the wedding. If you wait, you may have to scramble to find the dress you want and pay extra in alterations and rush fees that could have been avoided with planning. A good rule of thumb is to buy the dress that best fits you now and you can always alter it down if you lose weight. If you don't, you don't have to stress out. Remember, your gown can be altered to fit you perfectly and your fiancé loves you just as you are. Don't forget that you'll relieve a lot of the stress of planning your wedding once you have your dress (since you'll be able to focus on the many other decisions that go into planning your wedding) and a knowledgeable and competent seamstress can sculpt the dress you've chosen to fit you like a glove.

Myth#5 You shouldn't buy the first dress you try on at the first store you've gone to. This common belief is really an extension of Myth #3 that you have to look and look until you find the perfect dress. While it is a good idea to look to ensure that you make the best choice (it is your wedding after all), it is a myth to believe that you can't buy a dress you love at the first store you've been to. After all, you have great taste and are going to pick beautiful dresses from any store that you visit. A large percentage of brides end up buying the first dress they try on for this reason. Their eye is drawn to a dress they really love and they end up getting that first dress they tried on. Those brides who are indecisive usually come back and end up buying that dress after they've spent time and money on gasoline by driving all over that they could have easily saved by trusting their instincts and getting the dress they loved when they first tried it on. Trust your instincts. You may not find your dress at the first store you go to, but if you do, don't hesitate to begin enjoying the euphoric feeling you'll have knowing that you have that part of your wedding all taken care of. Remember, when you choose to bring lots of friends to help you shop, you also bring lots of opinions. Be careful that you don't let the opinions of your friends influence what you really want to wear (because, after all, it is your wedding).

Myth #6 If it is meant to be, it won't be sold before I come back. It is easy to get caught up in the notion of fate and that things happen for a reason. The opposite is also true. Sometimes things happen for no reason at all and for reasons that can't be explained. When you find your dress, it is best to decide to get it then, instead of letting another bride and her mother decide for you. At our store, we dress thousands of brides each year. We are busy and on multiple occasions we've seen brides who have trusted fate wake up to the realization that the dress they loved most had been sold. They cried, pleaded and begged for us to help them get another dress in, but many times it just isn't possible. The question you have to ask yourself is this: If you've found your dress, why would you let another bride and her mother tell you what you will or won't be wearing your wedding day? Isn't that a decision you'd rather make? Believe me, you don't want to return to a store you've been to hoping your dress is still there and leaving crushed that it has already been sold. We've seen that happen on too many occasions and we don't want to see it happen to you. When you find your dress, take control. Don't let the dress of your dreams slip through your fingers and let someone else make the decision for you. You've done the hard work and found your dress. Go ahead and get the dress you love and you'll be absolutely ecstatic leaving the store that no one can take the dress you've found away from you. On top of that, you'll save money by buying your dress on your first visit. You can use that savings for something else that you're planning for your wedding. Don't let the myth of fate determine the consequences of your decisions for you. You decided to marry your best friend and you should also decide to get the dress you love (not let someone else make that decision for you).

Myth #7 It's cheaper if you or someone you know makes your wedding dress. There is an old myth that says, "The bride should not make her own wedding dress; for each stitch up of the wedding garb the bride sews herself she'll shed one tear during her marriage." This old saying obviously has no scientific basis. While it is usually cheaper to do things yourself, such is not the case today with wedding gowns. All wedding gowns are sewn by hand and are done so by artisans and professionals who have years of experience in constructing gowns day in and day out. There are many intricate details that go into making a wedding gown. On some of the dresses in our store, there are over 10,000 individual beads that are sewn onto each individual dress, all by hand. It takes 38 days for one highly skilled seamstress just to sew on all of the beadwork, not to mention all of the other aspects of delicately placing each piece of boning and fabric to make a work of art. If you are blessed to have a talented seamstress in your family, you are a lucky bride indeed. However, even talented seamstresses recognize that wedding gowns that are produced at the best factories have a level of detail and attention that even they can't match or re-create. At our store, we are able to offer gowns at prices much lower than what a close family member can make a gown for (especially if you factor in all of the time it takes to create the gown and do all of the fittings). Do yourself a favor and let that special someone in your life help you do the alterations and trust the wedding artisans who construct our gowns to take care of all of the details to make your stunning dress. Regardless of this advice, many brides still choose to have someone else make their dress only to discover weeks before the wedding that it didn't turn out right or fit correctly. In the end, they've had to scramble to get a different dress (causing tremendous stress and anxiety). Don't let this happen to you.

Myth #8 Buying a dress online will save you money. This is a common perception of many brides who mistakenly believe the price they see online means everything else that will happen in the process of getting a wedding gown will be the same too. What happens when you buy a dress online versus buying it at a full-service bridal salon and it is dramatically different. We recently had a bride named Jessica who experienced this dramatic difference first hand. She came into our store in tears because the dress she received looked completely different than the picture she saw online. The lace was different, the seams were loose and crooked, there was no boning or support, and the dress bulged in certain areas. The company she purchased the dress from wouldn't refund her money and she was left to either fix what she had (which didn't give her a lot of options) or buy a new dress. She ended up buying a new dress at our store and wished she had done that in the first place. When you buy a dress from a full service bridal salon, you'll notice that:

- Your dress will be perfectly altered to your figure and pressed so that it is wrinkle-free and looks absolutely stunning on your wedding day. An online purchase will arrive wrinkled in a box and you'll have to pay more to have it pressed.

- Any beads that may have come loose during shipping or the alterations process will be tightened at no charge. An online purchase leaves you on your own. You'll have to pay to fix any beads that are loose or that have popped off.

- You can be assured that there won't be any spots or stains on your dress when you pick it up. For example, every dress we sell goes through our comprehensive 5-point premium care treatment process. When you purchase a gown online, you really don't know what you'll get. A dress purchased at a full service bridal salon ensures you'll get exactly what you thought and more.

- Your dress will be perfectly altered to your figure and you'll know that it will come in the right size. Buying a dress online is a gamble because you don't know if the size chart you saw online will really match the dress you're buying. At a full service bridal salon, what you see and experience will change your belief about buying anything online ever again.

- Lastly, your dress will look like the sample you ordered it from and you won't have to worry about any of the details.

With all that you have to worry about with planning the wedding of your dreams, you really don't need the extra stress and hassle of worrying that your dress may not come in correctly or be perfect for your wedding day. Why take the risk? When you order your gown from a full service bridal salon, you can be assured that we'll take care of all of the details. You'll be glad you did because you won't have to stress about the mess that could have happened with your dress.

Myth #9 If you don't cry, it's not "the" dress. Emotions are felt differently by people in varying situations. Not everyone cries when they see a touching movie or hear a tragic or moving story. The way you'll feel when you find "the dress" will likely be very different from how a well meaning friend or family member may have felt when they found their wedding gown. Just because they may have cried when they found their dress, doesn't mean that you will as well. Less than 30 percent of the thousands of brides we've helped to find their dress have cried when they made their decision. Instead of crying, these brides typically feel very excited and love to move around in their gown. They become possessive of the gown they're in and visualize themselves getting married on their wedding day. Another part of this myth is that if everyone in your wedding party doesn't like your dress, you shouldn't get it. The reality is, it is your wedding and it should be your choice.

Myth #10 It is better to order a dress than to purchase an in-stock dress. Some brides believe this myth because they think or feel that the dresses they try on at a bridal store have also been tried on by "hundreds" of other brides. This is very unlikely since most bridal retailers bring in brand new gowns to their stores several times each year and they are constantly refreshing their inventory to showcase the latest trends and fashions that brides in their respective areas are looking for. Since this is the case, the dress you try on has likely only been tried on by a handful of brides who all did so under the careful direction and supervision of their bridal consultant (so as to preserve the delicate detail, beadwork and fabric of each gown which is sold to and worn by a bride). This is another reason why it is such a good idea to be decisive when you find the perfect dress. We've seen brides come back extremely frustrated and disappointed because the dress they loved was purchased by another more decisive bride literally hours after they left the store. Don't let that happen to you. Another reason why it is a good idea to buy your dress when you find it out of stock is because there is an extra shipping, handling, and processing fee to order in a gown this way. Most bridal retailers get special incentives and pricing on gowns when they purchase in bulk and those same savings aren't available to them if they are only purchasing one gown just for you. You can avoid this extra cost by simply purchasing the gown you found on your first visit. If you have you heart set on special ordering a gown that will be made for you, we will be happy to assist you in making this happen. If you choose to order a dress, remember to plan plenty of time to order as outlined in myth #2.

CHAPTER 5

THE MYTH OF THE $99-$300 WEDDING GOWN

HEATHER AND JIM BUTLER

Following engagement, many brides discover that things are much more expensive than they thought they would be, particularly when it comes to a wedding dress. Many brides today come into bridal salons saying they have budgeted two or three hundred dollars on the low end for a wedding dress and maybe up to five hundred dollars on the high end. They are shocked to find the nearly impossible task of finding a well-made dress in this price range.

Most brides who have insisted on finding a dress in the $99 to $300 price range have found quickly that not all dresses are created equal. Those brides who are so set on a low-end price often end up spending more money on alterations than they did on the price of their dress because it is so inexpensively made.

In fact, most gowns that are sold for less than $600 that you see heavily advertised and promoted by the big box retailers are made from synthetic fabrics that have minimal construction details and are made this way by the store's request to their manufacturer to cut costs. These dresses usually don't have underlining, have minimal boning (if any at all) and are missing other structural supports to help the dress fit properly. These supports are extremely important as both boning and underlining fabrics help to hold the bodice of a dress up and securely in place. They also help provide a smooth fit over the bodice of the dress. If a dress doesn't have boning or good lining, you will see more wrinkles and crinkling of the fabric in a wedding dress. The last thing a bride wants to see in her wedding dress is bulges in the fabric of her dress due to minimal boning and lack of inner construction.

If you have been feeling stressed by the cost of your wedding and in particular the dollars you've budgeted for your wedding dress, this chapter we've written is just for you. We'd hate for you to make a mistake with such an important purchase that will be one of the focal points of your big day (especially since everyone will see you in it and will comment on how you look).

In this chapter, we'll explore how myths like the $99 to $300 wedding dress have appeared and why wedding dresses cost what they do. We'll also share with you several insights into how wedding gowns are constructed so you can be sure you are getting the best value for your money.

The initial sticker shock of wedding dresses may have come as a surprise to you. Why does a dress you'll wear one day of your life seem to cost so much?

There are four reasons and they all encompass various aspects of how the dress is made.

The first reason is fabric. This is what makes up the majority of the dress. Within each type of fabric, there are also many different grades or quality of fabric. Dresses can be made of silk, various types and varying grades of satin, chiffon, and organza. Many dresses today are also draped with exquisite lace.

Most moderately priced wedding gowns ($600 to $2000) are constructed from much higher quality fabrics and ornamentation and use higher grade fabrics that drape more elegantly and show off their versatility in design. The ornamentation and beading that is sewn onto these dresses is also of a much higher quality. There are varying degrees of inner construction and most dresses in this price range are fully underlined for stability and to give your finished dress a smoother appearance as it drapes across your figure. These dresses usually have some crinoline built into the skirt to provide additional support to that part of the dress.

As we mentioned, a very important part of the fabric that makes up a wedding dress is its lining. Lower priced gowns usually don't have any lining at all. As the price of wedding dresses increases, you'll find variations in the transparency and opulence of the fabrics that are used. In fact, some of the fabrics used for the inner lining on more expensive or couture dresses could be used as the outer fabric of many beautiful gowns. The difference in the thickness, thread count, and overall quality of the lining makes a huge difference in how well the dress flows, and most importantly, fits. Gowns that have very inexpensive lining often cause the outer part of your dress to make creases in the dress that won't flatter your figure.

Many dress manufacturers and big box retailers are able to offer dresses for seemingly low prices by cutting corners with less expensive dress linings or by using no lining at all underneath a dress.

Probably the biggest thing you'll notice when looking at the inside of a wedding dress that indicates high quality and construction is our second reason. It involves how the inner bodice of a wedding dress is made. The most expensive and highest quality gowns often have a built in bustier with boning that will flatter the figure of anyone in the dress. Some of these gowns are quite elaborate and exquisite. When you come in for your bridal appointment, please ask to see the inner construction of the gowns. You'll be amazed by the attention to detail and the way a well-constructed dress will fit on you. In fact, many brides admit that this is what draws them to buy one dress over another – how it fits and how they feel in it (which is all influenced by the inner construction of a gown).

The third thing that makes up the cost of the wedding gown is the time and skill it takes to make it. There are literally hundreds of hours of work in the construction of every single wedding gown we sell at our store. It is easy for some brides to want to buy a wedding gown for a price of $99 or $299 without having any consideration for the amount of time and the sheer talent that goes into constructing, and hand-stitching every bead and bit of appliqué onto a dress. Consider a dress that sells at a bridal salon for $700 to $1500. When you look closely at what goes into the construction of each gown, you will be absolutely amazed and floored by how inexpensively you can wear such a beautiful work of art on your wedding day. As we mentioned in Chapter 4, it takes one highly skilled seamstress thirty-eight days to sew on more than 10,000 beads on one bridal gown!

To appreciate the level of skill and workmanship this requires, time yourself sewing fifty beads (in three different colors) onto a piece of fabric in just a straight line, much less an intricate and beautiful pattern. How long would it take you to sew on these fifty beads? You can't make a mistake and put two of the same colored beads together and the beads must be sewn on by hand, one-by-one. Once you have spent a few minutes threading a needle, sticking yourself with the needle, having the needle get unthreaded again, etc. you really begin to appreciate the talent and skill the dressmakers have who construct by hand the beautiful gowns you see in a bridal salon like ours.

The skilled professionals who sew each and every dress we sell have spent years mastering their craft and take tremendous pride in their work. Shopping for a dress with only a dollar number in mind, discounts the tremendous efforts that are put forward by skilled professionals who have dedicated themselves to true mastery.

Most inexpensive wedding gowns that are priced under $500 are often made by less skilled artisans who are just beginning the process of learning how to make wedding gowns.

The fourth aspect of what makes up the overall cost of a wedding dress is its ornamentation. In fact, much of a gown's personality is made up in the type and amount of ornamentation it has. Dresses are often adorned with seed pearls, Swarovski crystals, and exquisite appliqués with corresponding beading. A big part of the cost of a wedding dress (especially the most expensive ones) is the quality of the little details that make up your dress.

One of the biggest aspects of ornamentation is the train of a wedding gown. Anciently, the length of the train was an indication of the amount of wealth the bride's family possessed. The longer the train, the wealthier you were. It was a status symbol and a way to show off your wealth to those who were invited to the wedding. Today, the type and length of train is most likely an indication of the formality or informality of the wedding. Longer trains tend to be more formal and less formal gowns typically have smaller court or sweep trains.

Since there are many types of ornamentation, I would recommend that you settle on a silhouette or cut before you consider all of the different types of ornamentation. The fit is really one of the most important features you should consider. Then, you can find a dress in that cut with the ornamentation that will best set the tone you want to create at your wedding.

That's it. Those are the four biggest things that make up the price of a dress. Now, when you go to a bridal store, you'll know why dresses cost what they do. You'll also understand the myth of the $99 wedding gown. This myth has been primarily promoted by big box retailers who use this low, low price as a tantalizing hook to get you to come into their stores. In reality, there are usually very few if any wedding dresses in that price range that are also in your size. And more importantly, you won't likely like the cheap dress for a lack of one of the reasons mentioned above.

How much you end up spending on your dress is completely up to you. We hope that this chapter has been helpful to you in determining why a dress costs what it does so you can be more realistic in your budget assessment for your dress. Nothing is more frustrating for a bride who drives to every bridal shop and spends hundreds of dollars in time and money and gas looking for the perfect dress for $100 that doesn't exist. A bride may be super-focused on finding a dress in this price range and then be devastated later to find that she spent more on alterations to fix the dress to fit her figure. She could have had the dress she really wanted if she would have budgeted a little more and got what she really wanted that fit her right in the first place. There is no reason for you to make this same mistake.

CHAPTER 6

NARROWING DOWN NECKLINES

HEATHER AND JIM BUTLER

The neckline is the feature most brides focus on after choosing the silhouette of their gown. Your neckline will have a strong impact on your appearance. It is the part of the dress most people spend time looking at and the one that draws attention to the face, collarbones, and décolletage. Since it is such a prominent feature of the gown, many brides rely on the neckline to add character to a gown or to highlight a unique feature of their figure. Here are the most common necklines and things to consider and avoid with each.

The neckline you choose should also flatter your face shape. You will still want to try on several necklines to find out what flatters your figure most and what you feel prettiest in. Talk with your bridal consultant about the neckline that may work best for you.

NECKLINE STYLE	PICTURE	GOOD FOR	NOT SO GOOD FOR
Halter Sleeveless style that fastens at the back of the neck and leaves the shoulders (and sometimes back) bare		Great shoulders	Broad or narrow shoulders
Off-the-Shoulder A slightly curving neckline that extends from shoulder to shoulder and features a small sleeve or fabric that lightly drapes over the shoulders		Medium to full sized bust and pear-shaped figure (smaller on top, heavier on the bottom)	Broad shoulders and thin hips
Scoop Features a softly curved line that gently slopes downward across the bodice		Everyone	
Spaghetti Strap Has very thin straps that go over the shoulders		Small to medium bust	Large bust or broad shoulders
Strapless The shoulders are completely bare. The bodice is usually cut straight across but can have varying necklines as well		Broad shoulders	Smaller bust (unless wearing push-up bra)

NECKLINE STYLE	PICTURE	GOOD FOR	NOT SO GOOD FOR
Square Features a square or rectangular shaped neckline		Well-endowed (cuts low but is not revealing) or LDS temple-ready brides	Hardly anyone
Sweetheart Features a graceful, open neckline that is shaped like the top half of a heart		Medium to large bust as the neckline curves down across the bust and comes to a point at the décolletage. (This causes a well-endowed bride to look better proportioned and is a tasteful way to display décolletage.)	Small bust
Tank Has no sleeves and can have either a scoop or V-neckline		Brides with muscular arms	Those with arm issues
V-Neck This neckline dips down in a flattering V. This elongates the neckline and de-emphasizes the bustline		B or C cups	Anything smaller or larger (the bodice will seem too empty or too full)

CHAPTER 7

THE LONG AND SHORT OF TRAINS

HEATHER AND JIM BUTLER

Much of a gown's personality is found in the skirt and train. Simply put, the train is the elongated back portion of the dress that stretches and trails out beyond the back of the skirt as you walk and move. The type and amount of fabric can add length, flair, and volume to give your dress a majestic touch.

Anciently, the length of the train was an indication of the amount of wealth the bride's family possessed. The longer the train, the wealthier you were. It was a status symbol and a way to show off your wealth to those who were invited to the wedding. Today, the type and length of train is most likely an indication of the formality or informality of the wedding. Longer trains tend to be more formal. Different types of trains can be a fun way to express your personality and style as you move throughout your wedding day.

Here are some of the more common types of trains and brief descriptions of each one. Try on several types of trains after you have determined which gown silhouette fits you best and makes you feel the prettiest. Most wedding gowns you will encounter in your search for "the perfect dress" will be sweep or chapel length.

Types of Trains	Example	Description
Sweep		This is the shortest type of train. It usually extends only 1 to 1 ½ feet beyond the end of the bottom of the dress.
Court		The court train extends the same distance as the sweep train but it extends right from the waist.
Chapel		The chapel length train is the most common on wedding gowns. It extends 3 ½ to 4 ½ feet from the waist to the floor.
Cathedral		A cathedral train extends 6 ½ to 7 ½ feet from the waist to the floor. It is typically very formal and requires extensive supporting bustles because there is so much material.

Types of Trains	Example	Description
Removable Train		For those who choose to have a very active reception, many brides choose a removable train. This way they can still have the train for the formal ceremony and pictures, but can remove it for the reception and dancing.
Lace Inset Train		You can add a lot of dramatic flair to a dress with a lace inset train especially if the lace is a different color than the rest of the dress.
See Through or Cut Out Train		Many wedding gowns have see through trains with lace and embroidery sewn onto the tulle or organza overlays. They add a sense of distinction and formality to the gown.
Bubble Hem Train		A bubble hem train has fabric that folds up under the base of the dress and will add a very unique look to the train and can have other embellishments along the base of the dress.

Types of Trains	Example	Description
Monarch		This is a pretty rare train to see on wedding dresses in America. They are usually reserved for royalty and extend 12 feet or more from the waist. This is the type of train worn by Maria in "The Sound of Music". It is so large that it requires people to help carry the fabric as the bride moves anywhere.
Carriage Back Train		A carriage back train folds outward from the waistline to the bottom sides of the dress. It can consist of a single or multiple layers and adds a unique flair to the gown.

Trains can be bustled up by gathering up all of the material and securing it with buttons or hooks. Talk with your seamstress about the different types of bustles you can create for your gown. She will likely show you several examples and then allow you to choose the one you like best.

CHAPTER 8

To Be or Not To Be Formal (Questions about the Formality of Your Wedding)

Diana Ellingson

Are you dreaming of the special day you get married? Where, when, how, why...all the little questions and details that are flowing through your pretty bridal head! It can get to be overwhelming to even the most organized bride to be...hopefully this chapter will help guide you to make the decisions flow in the direction that you and your fiancé are comfortable with. Remember it is your wedding, so choose what you as a couple are comfortable with. One of the first things to establish is a budget, and who will pay for what. Come up with a dollar amount that is realistic based on everyone's contributions. On average, couples in the United States spend $26,800 for their wedding, and that does not include the cost of the honeymoon, engagement ring, or wedding planner. Contrary to belief, your bridal gown purchase is not the most expensive part when paying for a wedding, whether formal or informal! The reception is the single largest expense, followed by other wedding services.

Formal or Informal Wedding?

Choosing the formality of your wedding can be a difficult decision. Wedding formality is largely determined by the size of the wedding and it's location. The number of guests invited and the number of attendants will also be a factor in your decision as to a formal or informal wedding.

Formal weddings are more traditional, and have different etiquette than the informal weddings. Choices, choices, choices...the bride generally makes the majority of the choices, but over the past 25 years in this business, I am happy to say I have seen a lot more involvement with grooms helping make some key wedding planning decisions. Where, when, how, and why are questions that need to be answered as to the formality of your wedding. In a lot of cases, a professional wedding planner is needed for a truly formal wedding because the number of things to do are too overwhelming in the amount of time that the bride, groom, and other family members are able to devote to the wedding.

A formal wedding calls for good taste, glamour, and ultimate class. If you have champagne taste and a small budget, focus on the most important aspects like the site, the entertainment, and WHAT YOU ARE WEARING!!! Let the rest fall formally into place.

Formal Wedding Outline:

* 200-500 wedding guests

* Bride: White or ivory formal bridal gown with a long train and a fingertip or cathedral veil

* Groom: White tuxedo or black tuxedo with a white tie and vest or black tie and vest

* Four or more bridesmaids in floor length gowns, and four or more groomsmen in black tuxedos

* Four to eight ushers. One usher per every 50 guests (most weddings make the mistake of not having enough ushers, I have waited outside more than one church due to a slow moving entrance because of not enough ushers!)

* Elaborate, professionally engraved wedding invitations on heavy card stock with accompanying response cards

* Ceremony site can be a church, synagouge, cathedral, or formal hotel

* Traditionally extravagant flowers decorating church, reception and carried by bride and her attendants, groom and his attendants wear fresh boutonnieres

* Wedding reception at an exclusive country club, exquisite hotel, or reception hall

* Full orchestra or band (Harp player for background music during dinner)

* Appetizers served before meal

* Formal "sit down" dinner (two or more meal choices with a menu on the table)

* Open bar with champagne and mixed drinks

* Elegant chair covers and place cards at the table settings

* Seating chart for all guests

* Draped ceilings with tulle or chiffon, and sparkling with twinkle lights

* Wedding favors decorating the table settings

* Tiered wedding cake and chocolate "groom's cake"

* Ice sculpture for decoration, or an "ice sculpture bar"

* Champagne toast done by the best man

* Wedding programs professionally printed

* Pew cards for ceremony seating

* Table settings of china service and beautiful plate chargers for decoration

* Rehearsal and formal grooms dinner the evening before the wedding

* Limousine for transporting bride and groom and wedding party from ceremony to reception

A semi-formal wedding calls for good taste, flair, and enthusiasm! Focus again on WHAT YOU ARE WEARING!!! Your Bridal Gown will set the direction on everything else that follows, bridesmaid gown styles, men's formalwear styles and colors, decorations, etc.

Semi-Formal Wedding Outline:

* 100-250 wedding guests

* Bride: White or ivory bridal gown with a chapel train and an elbow or finger-tip length veil

* Groom: Black tuxedo with black tie and vest

* Three or fewer bridesmaids in floor length or tea length gowns and three or fewer groomsmen in black or grey tuxedos with tie and vest to accent the bridesmaid gown color

* Two to five ushers--one usher per every 50 guests

* Printed wedding invitations on white or colored paper

* Fresh or silk flowers decorating church, reception and carried by bride and her attendants. Groom and his attendants wear fresh or silk boutonnieres

* Wedding reception in church reception hall or smaller reception hall

* Music D.J. service or single musician

* Buffet dinner

* Wedding cake, smaller tier design and sheet cakes for serving

* Wedding programs printed from your computer

* Rehearsal at ceremony site and groom's dinner at restaurant or groom's parents home

* Rental car or friends classic car for transportation from ceremony site to reception site

An informal wedding does not necessarily mean it is going to be less expensive...I have attended informal weddings that far outspent several of the formal weddings I have attended. Again, it is all in what you decide. An informal wedding can be more fun than any other type of wedding. Having fewer guests means that most of them will be your close friends and family.

When you have an informal wedding, it does not mean that the gown has to be "cheap & ugly" and informal does not mean the groom can show up in jeans...it means that you do not have to go the full formal route. I have personally helped several brides that choose to wear a bridal gown with a long train and finger tip veil on a beautiful sandy beach, in a court house, or in a back yard wedding! They all looked beautiful! Their photos in their bridal gown are amazing! Remember, your bridal gown is the most important clothing item you will ever wear, so go for it, look your best! You can also opt for simpler fabrics and dresses that may be more in tune with your style, size and body shape. Accent your best body features, and don't be afraid to ask your bridal consultant for help choosing the most flattering gown for your body shape.

Informal Wedding Outline:

* 50-100 wedding guests

* Bride: white or ivory floor length or gown with a chapel train or tea length bridal gown with a short veil.

* Groom: tuxedo in black or grey with a black tie and vest

* Maid of honor and no more than one bridesmaid, bestman and no more than one groomsman

* Two ushers--one usher per every 50 guests

* Invitations printed, handwritten, or over the phone

* Moderate fresh or silk flowers decorating church, reception and carried by bride & her attendants, groom and his attendants wear fresh or silk boutonnieres

* Reception at restaurant or in a home or backyard

* Light lunch, or light dinner (sometimes a coffee and cake only reception)

* Tables and ceiling decorated with crepe paper and balloons

* Small cake for bride and groom, sheet cakes for serving guests

* Cash bar.

* Wedding programs printed from computer

* Rehearsal at ceremony site and groom's dinner in groom's home/ yard or in a park

Of course, it's your wedding, so feel free to mix and match different ideas that you are comfortable with. If you want a formal wedding with 50 guests, go ahead. These guidelines are not written in stone, and you will want to add your own flair to your day! The main thing is that you choose what you like and choose the bridal gown YOU FEEL GREAT IN!!!

CHAPTER 9

The Fabrics That Make Up Wedding Dresses and How to Pick the Best One for Your Wedding

Heather and Jim Butler

The same dress style can look and feel quite different in a different color or fabric. In the search for your wedding gown, you'll want to try on several different dresses so you can find the perfect fabric and the most flattering color to match your complexion. Here are four tips to consider when shopping for the gown of your dreams with particular emphasis on fabrics and color.

1. Consider the overall feel that you want your gown to create at your wedding.

Your dress will set the tone and theme of the entire wedding more than any other single thing. What do you see when you close your eyes and imagine your wedding day? Are you going to be walking down an aisle, getting married outside or uttering your vows by the soft glow of candlelight? How do you want the fabric to drape across your figure? Do you want the fabric to shine or shimmer? If you're not sure, try on several types of fabrics so you can find out what you like best.

2. Try on several different fabrics and find out what complements your figure and taste.

The fabric of a wedding gown is the basis for its overall look and feel and will influence cost more than any other single thing. Here are some of the more common fabrics that you will have to choose from as you search for the "perfect gown":

Chiffon

- **Chiffon** is a thin, transparent fabric that can be made out of nylon, poly, silk, or rayon. It drapes very nicely and has a soft, romantic feel. It is much lighter than the other fabrics and is a great overlay on satin dresses or skirts.

Organza

- **Organza** is a sheer fabric that is crisper and heavier than chiffon. It shines and shimmers in the light and can make the dress "light up" in your bridal portraits. Organza is primarily used for layering and overlays on skirts.

Satin

- **Satin** is a smooth weave fabric that has a sheen or lustrous gloss on one side. It is typically made from acetate, poly, silk, or other manmade fibers. The majority of wedding gowns today are made from some kind of satin. More expensive gowns will be constructed from Italian matte satin, duchesse satin, or silk satin.

Tulle

- **Tulle** is a machine made crisp, netting-like material that is used for veils, ball gown skirts, and underskirts. It is what makes dresses 'pouf' out. Most brides either love tulle or they hate it. You'll have to try it on for yourself to find out how you feel about it.

Taffeta

Silk

Other materials from which dresses are made include a myriad of fabrics such as charmeuse (smooth, semi-lustrous soft weave fabric that is similar to satin but lighter in weight), **duchesse satin** (smooth, glossy, lustrous weave fabric), **damask** (fabric with interwoven floral or geometrical designs), **dupioni silk** (silk fabric that is similar to shantung but has coarse fibers and glossy sheen), **georgette** (sheer fabric that has a crepelike texture), **shantung** (similar to raw silk yet has a distinct nubby texture due to thick and thin threads and is lighter and more fine than dupioni), **taffeta** (stiff, crisp fabric that has a dull finish or sheen) and **velvet** (plush and thick weave felted on one side and plain on the other which is often embossed or patterned and is most often used as an accent - such as a sash).

3. Consider your complexion when selecting the color of your gown.

Even though white has traditionally been the color of most gowns, more and more gowns are being designed with color in the details. Many off white, ivory or rum pink/champagne colored dresses may be the perfect way to complement your complexion. Fairer skin tones look better in ivory or creamier tones since they often have a softer look against your skin in comparison with the stark contrast you may find with whiter fabrics. Many bridal stores will have the same dress style in either white or ivory and may have the dress with colors that are hand painted or woven into the fabric so you can get a sense for what you like best. Although having color in your gown may seem pretty fashion forward, consider that the colors on your gown can tie in corresponding colors for your reception or bridesmaid dresses.

4. Don't get so caught up in all the details that you forget how you feel and look in the dress.

There are so many fabrics to choose from. Don't let yourself get overwhelmed and confused. Just remember to choose a color and fabric that best reflects the mood you are trying to create at your wedding. Knowing the types of textured materials that are available can help you look for and create a special look for your dress. You will want to try on a variety of gowns to help you find what you like best as you bring "the perfect gown" into closer focus. As you decide on your gown, trust your own instincts. Ask yourself these three questions of the final dresses you are seriously considering: 1) Which dress do I feel the prettiest in? 2) which dress accentuates my best feature? and 3) Which dress most fits my personality or style? Try on each gown and go through this process until you have eliminated all of the dresses to the final one. Once you've found a gown that is everything you've imagined, smile and relax--you've done it!

CHAPTER 10

EXTRA EMBELLISHMENTS

(APPLIQUES, BEADING, BONING, BORDER TRIM, BOWS, CORSET, EDGING, EMBROIDERY, FRINGE, INSERT, KEYHOLD, LASER CUT, OVERLAY, PAILLETES, RUCHING, SEQUINS, ETC.)

BRENDA NORMAN

Embellishments on a wedding gown are like the icing on your wedding cake. They are the finishing touches that make each gown unique, and allow each bride to express her own individual sense of style.

Throughout history, many brides have used embellishments to show their personalities or their heritage. Queen Victoria added fresh orange blossoms to her gown in 1840. Jacqueline Kennedy wore her grandmother's heirloom rosepoint lace veil in 1953. In 1981, Princess Diana had over 10,000 hand embroidered pearls and sequins on her pure silk gown, complete with a twenty-five foot train.

To begin with, wedding gowns are made from the finest fabrics: beautiful satins, flowing chiffons, luxurious silks, and crisp taffetas. Many current fashion trends allow the fabric itself to actually become part of the embellishment. From ruching to origami-like tucks and folds, many gowns feature nothing more than artfully designed fabrics.

Like a blank canvas, a beautifully designed wedding gown can be turned into a masterpiece with just the right embellishment. Here are a few of the most popular kinds:

Appliques: Fabric elements like flowers, ribbons, or cutouts stitched or embroidered onto a gown, sometimes raised

Beading: Pieces of glass, crystal, gems or other material sewn onto lace or fabric

Austrian Crystal: Lead crystal polished and faceted to reflect a full spectrum of light

Bugle Beads: Long tubular-shaped glass beads

Border Trim: Braided, ribboned, ruffled, or scalloped edging that provides a decorative touch

Bows: Used in various lengths and sizes, from one giant bow to a tiny shoestring

Buttons: Although normally functional, buttons may also be an embellishment, such as buttons covering the back zipper (These may be satin-covered, pearls, or crystals)

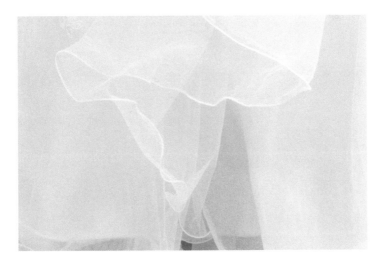

Edging: A narrow decorative border of lace, embroidery, braid, ribbon, or fringe used for trim

Embroidery: Fancy needlework patterns of various fine threads, sometimes metallic, done by hand or by machine

Flowers & Feathers: Small tufts of feathers added to a flower or lightly scattered over the skirt

Fringe: Ornamental trim consisting of loose strands of thread or beads attached to the main fabric of the gown

Seed Pearls: Tiny real or faux pearls used to adorn gowns, headpieces, and shoes

Baroque Pearls: Natural or faux pearls in irregular shapes

Sequins and Paillettes: Small, shiny, iridescent plastic discs sewn to fabric to add sparkle (Paillettes are a larger version and usually hang off the fabric adding movement as well as sparkle)

Many other embellishments may be added to your gown to make it personally yours. Other adornments to consider are belts and brooches.

Adding a belt to a simple gown can entirely change the look of a dress. Wide swiss double-faced satin in a matching or contrasting color creates a focal point and enhances the waistline. By adding a beautifully beaded belt you can give just that extra touch of bling to the dress.

Brooches can be added to belts, waistlines, and bodices. They can add a little sparkle or allow you to use a treasured family heirloom.

Now that you are well-versed in bridal embellishments, you're ready to go out and find the gown of your dreams.

CHAPTER 11

WHERE YOU SHOULD GET YOUR GOWN: THE INS AND OUTS OF A FULL SERVICE BRIDAL SALON

STACY VAN DUSEN

In today's society, there are many choices for where you could potentially shop for your wedding gown including online retailers, individuals selling their wedding gowns, used or rental gown retailers, businesses run out of a home setting, custom dress makers, big nationwide bridal stores, and last but not least, locally owned, full-service bridal salons. With all of these choices, it can often be confusing and overwhelming trying to decide the best place to shop while getting the best value for your money. This chapter will help you clarify your choices and show you that shopping with your locally owned, full-service bridal salon will save you time and provide you with the best overall value for your money.

Let's take a look at all of the options of where you could shop for your bridal gown. The next chapter will cover "Why Buying a Dress Online

Won't Save You Money", so we will look at purchasing your gown from an individual first. One of the main advantages to purchasing from an individual is to save money. But, will you really save as much as you think you will? If the gown has been previously worn, the gown may have some serious issues. Has the gown been altered to fit the previous owner? If so, can it be altered to fit you correctly without showing signs that it was altered? Who will alter your gown and do you trust them to do a good job? Wedding gown fabrics are not as durable as everyday clothing fabrics. The excessive altering of a wedding gown can permanently ruin the look of the dress. If the gown has been hemmed, unless extra seaming was left, it cannot be lengthened. Is the beadwork intact? Do you know where to purchase extra beads that match and how much does it cost? Manufacturers come out with unique beads and crystals every season that are difficult to find. A full service bridal salon would have easy access to purchase extra bead packets. Is the fabric snagged? If so, snags are permanent and cannot be removed. What about stains? Not all stains (including perspiration) can be removed in the cleaning process, and cleaning a wedding gown can cost $80-$150. Will there still be evidence or smells from the previous owner as you warm up and if you are nervous on your wedding day? If the gown you are looking at from the previous owner has never been worn, some of these issues can be avoided. But, they say that objects can take on energy from the previous owner. Do you really want the energy from a previous wedding gone wrong or failed marriage to mar your wedding day? You deserve to have a new gown that hasn't been previously worn or owned to set the tone for your new life. Create your day and your future around a gown that uniquely reflects you and your energy.

The second choice for shopping for your wedding gown would be to visit a used or rental retailer. Again, one of the advantages to shopping at a retailer offering used or rental gowns is to save money. For all of the same reasons as purchasing a used wedding gown from an individual, as well as the reasons that follow, you may not be saving as much money as you think you will. Most major manufacturers will not sell to a rental retailer. Therefore, the gowns offered at a rental store are used with all of the issues that have already been mentioned that arise from used dresses. Many brides like to have a bridal portrait taken ahead of their wedding or may be having more than one reception due to out of state family. Rental fees usually include one day rentals. How much extra will you be paying to have the gown an extra day? Will that gown be freshly cleaned ahead of your wedding? How is the gown altered to fit you? If the rental retailer leaves the seams in order to alter the gown for someone else, will those bulky seams show under the bodice? Will the hem look correct with extra seaming left for a taller bride? When you try on a rental gown, you will see the gown as it is today. What will the gown look like six months from now at your wedding? How many brides will have worn the dress by then? Is there a guarantee it will still be in good condition on your wedding day? What if you or one of your guests accidently damage the dress? Are you expected to pay for the gown or to pay a large damage fee? Who returns the gown to the rental place while you are on your honeymoon? When you purchase your new wedding gown from a full-service bridal salon, you will have your gown in hand, pressed and detailed to perfection. It will have been altered to fit your figure perfectly by the store or by a professional seamstress that the store trusts. You will have the dress of your dreams that will set the tone for your entire wedding.

The third choice for shopping for your wedding gown is to purchase your dress from someone running a home operated business. Again, the only advantage to shopping at a home operated business is to save money. The majority of home operated businesses only offer used wedding gowns. Most major manufacturers will not sell to a home-based business due to instability (they can disappear quickly if the home is rented) and the fact that they want the full-serviced retailer to represent their product. Many home-based business retailers do not take their business as seriously as a retailer with "brick and mortar" location. It takes a lot of discipline for someone working from home to meet deadlines and to stay on schedule. What guarantees do you have that everything will be done as promised? Is the home-based portion of the business separate from the actual home? Do they have set retail hours, or is it by appointment only? Can you get a hold of them by phone easily? What happens if you can't get a hold of anyone? Is that home-based business owner conscientious about food smells, pets, and children around your gown? How clean is their home and how do you know that your dress will be handled with care after you have left? Who is there to supervise or to fix any of these issues? Do you dare risk your wedding gown to the unknown?

The fourth option for shopping for your wedding gown is to have your gown custom made just for you. With this option, you really have to have a vision of exactly what you want in a gown, with the ability to communicate this need to a dress maker. It also incorporates having the knowledge of the designs and intricacies that go into the process of making a wedding gown. Custom making your gown will give you a unique dress that is exclusively for you. It does, however, come at quite a high price. Besides price, the main drawback to this process is the end result. Will it be exactly as you envisioned? Are there any guarantees if you don't like the gown? Will you be able to get your money back if you don't? Is the quality and workmanship of the dressmaker equal to what you would pay for a retail gown? What many brides don't realize is that there are usually several revisions made to a sample gown from a manufacturer before it is actually put into production. Extra care is paid by design teams to the draping, fabrics and quality of the dress before that final sample is produced and allowed to be sold to bridal salons. Because we have seen <u>many</u> last minute brides in our salons in tears about their custom made gown, it is always best to have a plan B if the custom dress you had made isn't what you thought it would be.

The fifth option for shopping for your wedding gown is to purchase your gown from a nationwide, big bridal retailer. Again, one of the biggest advantages to shopping at a nationwide, big bridal retailer is price. But is price really an advantage at these stores? Many times they will offer an advertised price that entices you into their store, such as $99, but this is for few, very shop worn dresses that may be restricted from being fixed or altered. When purchasing a discount gown from a full-service bridal salon, you are getting a unique wedding gown that is still high quality. It may have been discontinued by the manufacturer, but is still a current beautiful style. If altering the inexpensive gown is available, what is the pricing for this service? Does it put the price back up to what you would have paid for a gown through your full-service bridal salon? Alteration prices at the big bridal retailer may be double to triple the price for what you would pay at a full-service bridal salon or through a seamstress that the bridal salon trusts. The big bridal retailers also specialize in mid-range gowns priced at $400-$800. Are the gowns the same quality as those offered at a full-service bridal salon for the same price? You can judge for yourself by touching and looking at the fabrics, laces, embellishments, and internal construction offered at the big bridal retailer, versus the quality of the designer gowns found at your full-service bridal salon. You will find the better quality at the full-service bridal salon. Many of the fabrics offered at a big bridal retailer are purchased by the buyers because there is more profit from making mass produced gowns out of that fabric. These fabrics offered at the big bridal retailer may be unique, but not in a good way. Be sure to look at the fit of the gown and the way the fabric drapes and hangs. Is it a good quality fabric and is there enough lining and internal construction to make the gown lay appropriately? Often times your big bridal retailer will advertise a large selection in every size. But in reality, they offer the same 25-30 gowns in every size severely limiting your choice and increasing the risk that you will see your gown on another bride at another wedding because the store is nationwide. Does your big bridal retailer know the brides in your area? Your locally owned, full-service bridal salon will have years of experience catering to brides in the area, will know the trends, can often fulfill requests from the local bride, and will shop the major markets (Chicago, Atlanta, Dallas or New York) for the best dresses from hundreds of styles for their demographic. You will have access to the best of the best designs from the runway shows by shopping at a full-service, bridal salon. A local bridal salon may also offer limited edition gowns that are not seen at other bridals stores.

What happens if there are issues or problems when dealing with a big bridal retailer? Are these issues resolved at a local level, or do you need to deal with a nationwide office that is far removed from where you are? A full-service bridal salon will have an owner or manager on site to deal with any issues directly and quickly. They also care because they have a personal stake in the outcome of any issue and pride themselves on customer service. What is the selection of veils, tiaras, floral head pieces, etc. like at the big bridal retailer? Your local, full-service bridal salon will offer better quality accessories at comparable, if not better prices because they have shopped the major bridal markets for the highest quality accessories for the best value for the local bride. The big bridal retailer will often offer financing, on approved credit. Do you really want to finance your wedding gown at a high interest rate in this economy? Your full-service bridal salon will usually offer a layaway program that is more flexible and of lower or no cost than a financing program without effecting your credit.

The last and best option in shopping for and purchasing your bridal gown is to visit your locally-owned, full-service bridal salon. When you purchase your gown from a local bridal salon, your dollars spent go directly back into the local economy by providing jobs. Any profits that business makes will also filter back into the local economy in the form of compensation for the employees and purchases made by that company's management for supplies. Economists have also said that the growth of small businesses will be the backbone for economic growth out of the recession. It is easier for a small business to respond to changes in its environment and customer requests than a large chain. Your local, full-service bridal salon will have also established relationships with other local, wedding retailers and may offer you discounts or coupons to help you with your wedding. Let's recap all of the above advantages to shopping with your locally-owned, full-service bridal salon.

- New, designer gowns at competitive prices

- Many, if not all, limited edition gowns not offered at other salons

- High quality fabrics, embellishments, beadwork and a superb fit

- Gowns that have been selected especially for brides in your area

- On-site owners and/or managers to pay attention to every detail

- Knowledgeable, professional bridal consultants who care about their brides and take pride in customer service

- Pressing, spotting and detailing your gown to perfection with exact beadwork

- Clean, controlled environment

- Selection of affordable, superior accessories

- Quick, complete, local resolution of any issues or problems

- Special relationships with other local retailers, with special coupons or discounts to purchase from those retailers

- Alterations in-house or recommended, trusted seamstresses to alter your gown to fit at affordable prices

- Money spent at locally-owned bridal salon benefits the local economy

In conclusion, shopping with your locally-owned, full-service bridal salon will give you that quality, wedding gown of your dreams at a competitive price while helping out your local economy. You can also be confident that you have made the best choice for value, quality, and selection along with the peace of mind that comes from working with the salon's dedicated managers and consultants who will focus their attention on ensuring that every detail of your purchase goes smoothly.

CHAPTER 12

WHY BUYING YOUR DRESS ONLINE WON'T SAVE YOU MONEY

HEATHER AND JIM BUTLER

Many brides today opt to buy their dress online after visiting numerous bridal stores. Since you may be considering this, you will want to read this article and the enclosed letter and pictures from a bride who made this choice. Here are several things you should consider that will likely cost you more money than originally anticipated and cause the savings you thought you were getting to completely vanish. We could tell you that you are making a mistake by choosing to buy online, but we won't. You'll realize it as soon as you open the box (or in Jessica's case as soon as she saw the box).

Here's what you'll notice:

- The dress will have wrinkles all over it which you will have to pay extra to have pressed out. Many bridal salons offer a free service to have this done with the purchase of a wedding gown. You may pay $60 to $80 or more to have this same service done at a dry cleaner or bridal salon.

- There may be loose beading or missing beading caused during shipping which you will have to pay to have fixed (most shipping companies aren't as kind to your box as you would like to think they are).

- There may be spots or stains on the dress that you likely won't be able to properly remove without damaging the delicate fabric and beadwork on the dress.

- The dress may come in the wrong size (and you may not be able to alter it to fit your figure).

- And lastly, you may order the dress and even if you get it, it may look completely different than the picture you saw online. Many brides have experienced this much to their shock and horror and then come to us in tears hoping that we can fix the problem. Many times repairs can be made, but often at a great expense.

We recently had a bride named Jessica come into our store who had purchased a wedding dress online. You can read her story in her own words on the next page. She was in tears because the dress she received looked completely different than the picture she saw online. The lace was different, the seams were loose and crooked, there was no boning or support, and the dress bulged in certain areas. The company she purchased the dress from wouldn't refund her money and she was left to either fix what she had (which didn't give her a lot of options) or buy a new dress. She ended up buying a new dress at our store and wished she had done that in the first place.

When you buy a dress from a full service bridal salon, you'll notice that:

- Your dress will be perfectly altered to your figure and pressed so that it is wrinkle-free and looks absolutely stunning on your wedding day.

- Any beads that may have come loose during shipping or the alterations process will be tightened at no charge.

- You can be assured that there won't be any spots or stains on your dress when you pick it up.

- Your dress will be perfectly altered to your figure and you'll know that it will come in the right size.

- Lastly, your dress will look like the sample you ordered it from and you won't have to worry about any of the details.

With all that you have to worry about with planning the wedding of your dreams, you really don't need the extra stress and hassle of worrying that your dress may not come in correctly or be perfect for your wedding day. Why take the risk? When you order your gown from a full service bridal salon, you can be assured that we'll take care of all of the details. You'll be glad you did because you won't have to stress about the mess that could have happened with your dress.

Here is the letter that we recieved from Jessica:

Dear Future Brides,

I'm writing this letter to inform you of the terrible mistake I made and hope to keep you away from doing the same. After realizing my budget was tight I decided to find my perfect dress online. I came across a web site that advertised my dress, it had the same picture form the [manufacturer's] website and said they had a 100% satisfaction guarantee.

I ordered my dress for $400 online, I waited about 6-8 weeks to receive the dress. I was so thrilled to have my dress. When I finally arrived home to see the package I knew there was something wrong just by the look of the package. The package was the size of a throw pillow you would have on your couch. I opened the dress & began to try it on. I had to do everything in my power to hold back the tears. The dress was a mess!

Once I had the dress on I could see the damage & the dress was nothing like the [manufacturer's] one they advertised on the web site. The beading on the bust was nothing like the beading from the [original manufacturer], I could see the tops of my feet, the dress was way too short. The dress was way too big & the lace was all pulled on the bottom. The zipper in the back had a gap in-between you could see my back through the dress. You could see the stitching in the front of the dress through the bunching. After all the wrong things with the dress I still had to try to have hope, so I took it to a well known seamstress just to see if it could be possible to fix this disaster of a dress. Sadly, she said there is nothing she could do, she would have to redo the entire dress! In her words, "the best thing you can do is either buy a whole new dress, or try & get your money back."

So with that I decided it was time to send the dress back. I went online to the web site. When I looked for the return address it gave me an email address to contact for further instructions & I also noticed on the top of the page it said: Returns can be done within 3 days from the date of receipt. After 3 days there will be no refunds or exchanges. In case of refund, 15% restock fees will be charged. We only accept returns if it has something wrong with the dress, like a manufacture damage. The buyer is responsible for all shipping costs, and they will not be REFUNDED.

I waited until the 3rd day of no response from the company & had to make a huge decision, should I send it back to China where it came from or "hope" someone is going to return an email? I couldn't wait any longer, I sent it back to China after no response. On the 4th day, I finally received a response simply stating: "Why?" No return address, they gave me absolutely nothing.

My mom tried going through the credit card company to get more answers & our money back, but since we sent it back so quickly we didn't think to take pictures of all the damage of the dress. The credit card company told us we were not getting refunded because we had nothing to show.

After about 10 weeks of no response from the web site we thought we were out of luck. Until I came home & received the same package I had sent to China.

Finally a glimmer of hope. We were already making payments for my original dress at your store. I asked the owner if she could please write me a letter for our credit card company explaining the horrible dress I received & the extreme differences between the 2. Luckily, she wants to show girls like me what a mistake it can be to buy your precious wedding gown online. She has brought my dress not to scare girls into buying her gowns but to save them from a huge stressful ordeal.

I hope I have saved you from the same drama I've been through. It's a lesson learned, I know I will NEVER buy anything so precious online again. My wedding day is worth more than saving a few dollars & I know that now. Through this letter I hope to help at least one beautiful bride on their special day.

Sincerely,
Jessica Girginis

Don't make the same mistake Jessica did. It isn't worth it for your wedding.

CHAPTER 13

WHO AND WHAT TO TAKE WITH YOU WHEN SHOPPING

SUE ROSENBERGER

The quest for your wedding gown can be one of the most exciting and fun filled parts of planning for your wedding. Your gown will set the tone for your entire wedding and there are few other times when you will be so lavishly pampered as you are magically transformed in to a beautiful bride before your very eyes. This can be one of the most memorable moments of the wedding experience. It will be a time for laughter and a time for tears. As you begin your quest for that special dress it will provide a wonderful opportunity for you to bond with the special women in your life.

SHOPPING TIPS AND GUIDELINES

Before you start shopping for your wedding gown consider the following tips and guidelines as you begin on your journey.

Gather ideas to create your vision for how your wedding will look. Consider the formality of the wedding. Will it be a candelight, formal event in a traditional church setting, a casual, outdoor or on-the-beach destination venue, or an over-the-top party celebration?

Take a moment and close your eyes. What do you envision, you as the bride wearing when you walk down the aisle to your groom? Once you have that vision, let that be a "starting point" on your journey to finding a wedding gown you will feel the most beautiful in and best fulfills your vision.

Most reputable bridal retailers require that an appointment be made in advance. Wedding gowns are delicate and fragile and will require the assistance of a knowledgeable consultant to assist you with the gowns.

For bridal retailers the busiest days are Friday afternoon, all day Saturday and often Sundays. The best time to shop is on a weekday. Your bridal consultant will have more "extra" time to spend with you than would be possible on a busy weekend. So when possible, take a shopping day off during the week.

Now you are armed with pictures of gowns, silhouettes you are drawn to and you are ready to call all your friends and invite them to come shopping with you as you search for your wedding gown.

WHAT TO BRING
Before you go dress shopping, make sure you're freshly bathed and scrubbed, and wear undies (no thongs, please!) Remember to wear nude undergarments. Seamless and nude-colored undergarments will lie flat and be undetectable under your dress and will prevent visible panty lines under figure-hugging gowns. Avoid hair spray and perfume, and don't apply hand or body lotion, unless it will have at least an hour to be absorbed. It's even more important to avoid tanning solutions. They can ruin a gown if the color smears. And ALWAYS leave food and drink outside the store.

The bridal store staff will wait on you more closely than you're used to when shopping for other clothing. It's their job to help you find the dress of your dreams; it's also their responsibility to be protective about the store's expensive, delicate merchandise. So don't feel crowded if a staff member comes right into the dressing room to assist you. Enjoy the attention!

WHO TO BRING WITH YOU

It is strongly recommended not to bring children or babies to a bridal store. If you or the friends who shop with you have children, arrange for a sitter. This needs to be stressed" *a bridal salon is NO place for children*. Your wedding gown choice is one of the most important decisions you will make for your wedding. For the rest of your married life you will be looking at pictures of yourself in that special gown. When shopping for your wedding gown you need to be able to focus and concentrate without distractions. A bridal salon is not a fun place for children and they will get bored very quickly. While the adults are looking at wedding dresses, a curious or bored child can cause hundreds of dollars in damages, or even get hurt due to loose pins and other hazards. It is natural for children to dance in front of the mirrors, be the center of attention and totally distract you from this important mission. Crying babies also distract other future brides on this most important day. If you want to shop for a flower girl dress, arrange a dedicated outing to focus on that, and make your flower girl feel like a princess for the day.

Sooo . . . who exactly *should* you invite to go shopping with you? Your friends and relatives are all jumping for joy and insisting on coming with you to find your gown. But wait a minute - just how big of a committee should you have for this project? What are their voting rights? Do they all have an equal say in what you will be wearing down the aisle? Will they all share your vision of your wedding? What about their taste in fashion - do they share *your* taste in fashion?

When shopping for a wedding gown all the experts advise not to bring an entourage. Shopping for your wedding dress is a special time that should be reserved for special people. Your mom and one or two other trusted individuals seem to be the perfect mix. You may want their opinions, but remember that their personal styles may be different from yours, and if so, take their advice with a grain of salt. Sales consultants cringe when thay have to battle too many bridesmaids' opinions. Too often the consultant has witnessed a bride brought to tears by her enterouge having many different opinions and making inappropriate comments and remarks at the brides expense. Don't turn this unique day in to a three ring circus. It's great to have one or two people who are close to you to give you honest opinions but bringing too many people to "poll the audience" is a recipe for disaster that may make you miss out on your perfect gown. Listen to your own instincts about what dress makes you feel the prettiest. It's easier to hear what your heart says if you don't have a crowd with you.

This is your decision, and you need to feel comfortable and look like yourself. If your style is simple, this is not the time to wear an overly beaded dress. Buy the dress you love. Not the one your mom, best freind and sales consultant love. You'll feel comfortable when it's right.

You want to look back at your pictures and love what you chose. Stay true to your personal style. Bring a few people who love you to come, and your experience will be a lot more enjoyable and you will have a better chance of being successful in your quest.

THE ONE!

In the end the only opinion that truly counts is YOURS when picking a wedding dress. You will be the center of attention at your wedding. You will want a wedding gown that will make you look awesome and feel amazing. You are the only one that will really know when you have found the gown that does this.

Once you've decided which dress is THE ONE, stop looking at other dresses! Don't try to second-guess yourself. Have faith in your own judgement, and enjoy the peace of mind that comes from having one of your most special decisions looked after.

CHAPTER 14

DRESSING IT UP
WITH ACCESSORIES

HEATHER AND JIM BUTLER

The accessories you wear with your wedding gown are critically important for making your transformation into a bride complete. You wouldn't dream of showing up at your wedding without your makeup and hair being done so don't get married without the proper accessories that match and complete your look. In this chapter, we'll share with you five tips for finding the perfect veil and tiara.

A veil is one of the final accessories that will make your transformation into a bride complete. It is most often made from varying lengths of tulle (a machine-made crisp, netting like material) and can have a wide assortment of embellishments which adorn its body and edges. Anciently, it was believed that the veil protected the bride from evil spirits. Most brides today wear the veil to top off the perfect dress in a fun, elegant and stunning way. Your veil can have a finished trim with piping (cording) or ribbon or can be unfinished and adorned with crystals, pearls or rhinestones.

Here are five things to do when searching for your veil & tiara:

1. **Pick your dress before you pick your accessories.** Many veils & tiaras match or have elements that can be found on the dress you choose. Picking accessories before you decide on the dress will most likely confuse you – since you'll be trying to match a style of veil and tiara to a type of dress that may or may not accentuate your best features. It is best to not even try on accessories until you've decided on your dress. Then you can focus on the color and other elements you love about your dress that you want to accentuate with the accessories you choose. The key is to consider what you like first, and then find a veil/headpiece that compliments your gown as close as you can.

Pick a veil and tiara that doesn't distract from you or from the dress. If your dress is really ornate and has a lot of beadwork or embroidery, it is best to wear a plain or simple accessories so that they don't distract from the dress. A plain dress looks great with a long cathedral length veil or a veil that is adorned with embroidery, lace or beadwork. Also, avoid veils that have really thick ribbons on the edging of the veil because they tend to divert the focus from your face to the veil. Some of the more common lengths of veils for you to consider are featured in the table below:

Lengths of Veils	Picture	Description
Waist Length		Veils can come with piping (cording), and ribbon along the edge of the veil. A waist length veil falls just below the waistline. Both of these veils have a blusher which is traditionally worn over the face during the ceremony and flipped over the head or removed after the wedding ceremony.
Fingertip Length		This veil extends to your outstretched fingertips. It is approximately 45-50 inches in length and can be single or double layered with a blusher front.
Waltz or Ballet Veil (Calf Length)		This veil falls between the knees and the ankle.
Cathedral Length		Cathedral veils are typically worn at formal weddings and can be so dramatic that they become the focus of your attire. If your dress is floor length, you may choose a cathedral veil to give the impression of a long train. The veil extends 3 ½ to 5 feet beyond the base of the dress.

Three other types of veils that you may also consider are:

- **Flyaway**– this veil is a shorter veil that just brushes the shoulders. It can be single or double-layered and is most often considered to be a less formal type of veil.

- **Mantilla** – this Spanish styled veil is long and has a lot of lace. It can be made entirely of lace or have heavy lace on the edge of the tulle.

- **Cage** – A cage veil is made up of tulle and lightly drapes around the face or over one eye depending on its placement. They are very elegant and dramatic and can be combined with feathers or flowers for a very distinguished look.

3. **Experiment with different placements of the veil, tiara or other accessories in your hair.** Most veils have a comb attached so the veil can easily be attached in your hair. Depending on how your hair is styled for the wedding, you may want to place the veil higher or lower on your head. As you examine how the veil looks from every angle, you'll be able to determine what fits you and the dress best. If the veil & tiara seem unstable, you can have your hairdresser secure the veil with bobby pins.

4. **Choose a style that best matches your face shape and body type.** A good rule of thumb is to pick a length and volume of veil that is the opposite of your face shape and body type. For example, if you have a round face, wear a longer veil that falls along the side of your face to balance and visually narrow your face. If you have an oval or oblong face, wear a poufy veil that will add width. A fluffy, poufy veil can overwhelm a petite bride, while this style of veil can give a taller bride a stronger presence. Try several types of veils on and look at them from every angle to determine what best fits your face and body type. If you aren't sure, ask a friend, family member, or your bridal consultant.

5. **Wear a tiara or headpiece to complement the veil.** A headpiece or tiara can complete your look and will most likely contain shapes or patterns of pearls, crystals or beads that will match your dress. Try on several tiaras to find one that will complement your veil placement and dress best. If you're not sure, ask your bridal consultant to help you find a specific tiara that matches your veil and dress. They work with dresses and veils all the time, so they will likely be able to help you find the perfect match.

CHAPTER 15

THE PROPER FOUNDATION (BRA/BUSTIER, SLIPS AND SLIMMERS, HOSE, UNDERWEAR AND SHOES)

PAM HENDERSON

Ahhh... the underpinnings....almost as important as the dress itself, are the undergarments that support the gown. Proper undergarments can accentuate your assets and de-accentuate your "distractions". Proper undergarments can turn a "so-so" dress into a "so-fabulous" dress!

Before getting into the details, it is necessary to discuss bridal gown SIZING. Bridal and formalwear sizing is very different than ready-to-wear sizing. So is fabrication. While you are super comfy in those size 6 stretch jeans from Nordstrom's, bridal size charts have not adapted to the growing American girth. Do NOT scream, panic or hit the road when your professional consultant measures you at a bridal size 12. Also, keep in mind that the fabric of most bridal gowns does not stretch. Unless you are intentionally buying a dress made of clingy fabric, such as stretch satin or charmeuse, your wedding gown will have little give. Another factor that you have to keep in mind is the bridal manufacturer's size charts. A common "problem" with wedding gown sizing is that the sizing is standard or average. This means that the dress is sized from typically three measurements, the bust, waist and hips. These measurements will determine your size, but not necessarily your SHAPE. Shaping of the dress to your body is usually done by a seamstress and can be helped with the proper underwear, most importantly the bra and petticoat. When ordering your size, the bridal consultant will take your measurements and compare them to a manufacturer's chart. Depending on your shape and the style of the dress, your professional consultant will usually use the largest measurement to determine your size. If your waist is the largest measurement, it is generally wise to order the dress using that measurement. If you waist size is bigger than the actual measurement of the dress, it doesn't really matter that the bust and hips fit if YOU CAN'T ZIP THE DRESS UP! Also keep in mind that hormone changes, pregnancy and the "Freshman 15" can effect the size of your dress. This applies to bridesmaid dresses as well as the wedding gown. Do not be in a panic when your bridesmaid calls, frantic because the bust of her dress is too big and the length too long—a common frustration. She was sized for her waist measurement, any smaller and the back of the dress wouldn't close. As for the length, unless ordering a custom length (cost prohibitive in most bridesmaid lines), her dress comes "standard". "Standard" meaning accommodating girls that are five feet 10 to six feet tall; it's easy and inexpensive to take off length, but nearly impossible to add length. I will never forget the mother of the bridesmaid who called, screaming, that we had mis-sized her daughter. She said her daughter was almost 6 months pregnant with her first baby and was ordering a non-maternity cut bridesmaid dress for her friend's wedding. The mother was screaming at us because the dress was a little too big for the now 8 ½ month pregnant girl and the bust had to be taken in. I can hardly imagine what she would have said, had the dress been unable to zip. Using the size chart, we had to guess what her expanding belly would be and order accordingly. The large waist measurement naturally meant that the bust would be large, huge, in this case because the girl was not ordering a maternity dress. Or what about the bridesmaid who INSISTED that she was a size 8, even though she fit perfectly in our size 10 sample...? She called AFTER the wedding complaining that the zipper had popped... Believe me, the bridal store is NOT ordering the dress too big so that they can make money on alterations—we wish it fit you perfectly too!

Now that you understand sizing we can go on to the topic at hand.

The BRA:

Lift those girls up! Many gowns, especially ones with full-embodied corseting have built-in bras. The closer the size fit, the better this feature will work. A fully corseted dress when zipped, buttoned, or laced will feel stable and not move away from your bust. Internal boning will support the bodice of your dress as well as the bust line and should sit firmly on your waist. Because the size of your dress was probably determined from the average size, unless you have a bra cup size of a DD, you will notice some gaping in the bust area. If this occurs, don't distress! No, your dress was not ordered in the wrong size, it just accounted for all your measurements as a whole, rather than just one measurement (a smaller bust related to the waist measurement). Wedding gowns manufacturers need to account for the biggest bust size possible in each given size standard because you cannot generally add fabric to the dress, but it's much easier to take the dress in. As mentioned before, most bridal shops will order from the larger measurement with the correct assumption that it is easier to have a seamstress take the dress IN rather than let the dress OUT. GENERALLY speaking, a bigger tragedy would be to order your dress using the smallest measurement (say the bust or the hips) and then not being able to zip the gown up! Yikes! Of course, every girl is built differently and a professional bridal consultant will be able to give you accurate advice about sizing your dress.

If you are not sure, your bridal consultant or seamstress can determine the best way to fix a gaping bust. If the dress if fully corseted with adequate internal stays (boning sewn into the lining of the bodice of the dress) you may not need a separate bra, but instead, bra cups. Bra cups are sold in pairs with or without silicone gel inserted in the bra cup. Bra cups are usually sewn into the dress by your seamstress. I much prefer bra-cups than a separate brassiere or bustier. Bra cups are hidden in the bodice of the dress and will not show, even with extreme movement. Bra cups are usually desirable for bra cup sizes of A-B-C-D. Also, bra cups work well if your "girls" are two different sizes. Bra cups can also be used to insert in regular bras for additional cleavage or for help post-mastectomy. Bra cups are also good at filling out the shape of a bodice when you don't necessarily need or want a bigger cup size. The most common alteration, besides a hem to the bottom of the dress, is the bust alteration. Often the best, simplest and least expensive fix to fitting the bust area is having the seamstress sew in a pair of bra cups and taking in the side seams just under the arms. Bra cups and under-the-arm alterations are the best way to prevent you from feeling like you need to pull your dress bodice up during the event.

Bras and bustiers are necessary if you do not feel that your gown has enough internal support to hold up your breasts even with the support of bra cups. Evidence of needing a bustier is sometimes manifested by the presence of a deep crease underneath the bust line when you are standing up straight (with good posture!) or if you feel like your breasts are sagging. If you feel like you need to pull the bodice of your dress up, or if it feels like the dress if dropping you need additional support. The phrase "you get what you pay for" strongly applies when buying a bra/bustier. Keep that in mind when trying on different styles and sizes. If you have a cup size larger than a D, you probably cannot get away with bra cups, so plan for a good bra in your bridal gown budget. If proper bust/bra support does not resolve the crease under the bustline you might want to consider putting straps on your dress which will usually solve the problem and give you additional bodice support. Spaghetti straps almost always come included with your strapless dress. They are not sewn on, but come separately to use or not use at your discretion. If you are not sure, ask your bridal consultant. Simple spaghetti straps are an easy way to secure the bustline for an absolute sure fix and an additional point of support (over the shoulder) for a trouble-some pair of bosom.

It stands to reason that if you are wearing a strapless dress, you should buy a strapless bra. Halter bras, may or may not work with a halter dress. Get the advice of your bridal professional or seamstress. Do not be tempted to wear the clear straps that sometime come with a strapless bra or bustier. The clear straps will show indentation on your shoulders in your pictures. When buying a bra for your most important dress, it is necessary to be sized professionally. I was amazed recently when I measured a different size than I had worn for years. A modest weight loss had decreased the cup size and increased the chest size! I was amazed at how much more comfortable the bra felt and fit. Skin bulges smoothed nicely INSIDE the bra instead of bulging OUTSIDE the bra. Yikes! I hope no one looked too hard at the gym!

Make sure that the bra doesn't show, especially when raising your arms. Another option is a stick-on bra. I don't like these as much as bra cups, but for some dresses it works perfectly. Use a stick-on bra if bra cups won't stay in place and a strapless bra shows. Stick-on bras are best used with deep cut "V" neck dresses made with flowy or clingy fabric that moves too much to keep sew-in cups in place. Newer version of the stick-on bra have self-stick adhesive, are made of silicone and are nude in color for a more natural look.

A bustier differs from a bra by supporting not only the breasts but extending down to the waist, and sometimes hips, with various degrees of compression. When wearing a bustier, the ribcage is supporting the dress rather than just the breasts. Bustiers come in different lengths, a shorter version extending only a few inches below the bust line and having a regular bra closure in the back to the longest version, sometimes called a "long-line". A "long-line" bustier can extend to and even over the hips and usually contains "stays" or plastic boning which helps considerably in slimming the waistline. If your usual cup size is larger than a D, consider using a bustier that has boning built into the CUPS as well as the length of the bustier.

The best way to shop for a bra or a bustier is after you have purchased and received your dress. Decide what you are trying to accomplish with the bustier. Do you need to support your breasts? Do your breasts need to be "enhanced"? Would you like your waist to appear smaller? Do you need your torso to be smaller to fit into the dress that you ordered a size too small because you thought you would lose weight or didn't believe the bridal consultant when she told you your size? Do you want something with minimal support that will look sexy underneath the dress (for the party that will take place after the wedding reception)? Keep all these things in mind when shopping for the bustier. Besides getting the proper fit, an important thing to think about when trying on a bustier, is making sure that it doesn't show. Small edges peeking out of the top of your dress can usually be easily solved by the seamstress. The seamstress can also shorten a long-line bustier if the stays are extending too far down your torso. For wedding gowns with minimal support, your seamstress might want to sew the actual bustier into the bodice of your gown. This type of alteration usually prevents the bustier from showing and gives the gown a better fit. When scrutinizing a bustier, also make sure that it doesn't show through the fabric of the dress in weird bumps created by the stays on the bustier. Be careful buying a bustier with lace, bows and buttons as those types of embellishments might also show through the gown as awkward looking lumps. Other things to watch for (or watch-OUT for) would be buying a bustier that fits too tight. If you are wearing a strapless dress, a too-tight bustier can push the skin folds up in the back area creating the dreaded "back fat". Sometimes "back fat" can be smoothed out by pushing the skin gently back into the bustier, but most often not.

I have found that even the most ambitious bustier will not take you down more than one size. The only product that can truly get you down more than one size is a French corset. This product is worn with your regular bra and wraps around your middle. Depending on your generation, think Scarlet O'Hara in *Gone With The Wind* or, for the younger set, Keira Knightly in *Pirates of the Caribbean*. The back is open and laces up the entire length. You will not be able to put on this product without help of a very, very, very, good friend. It is possible to lose several inches in your middle with a French corset but what you loose in inches will be sacrificed in comfort (and possibly health and safety!). Because this product has stays running up and down and all around, there is a possibility of bumps showing. In my professional opinion, it is much better to buy your dress in a bigger size than to try to torture yourself by wearing a French corset!

SPANX®!

Out with the girdle, in with the SPANX! If the story behind the creation of Spanx doesn't inspire you, the names of the products will. Names like Power Panties, Higher Power, and High-falutin' Footless will make you chuckle as you wiggle your way into Sara Blakely's revolutionary new product. Inspired by the lack of practical products, designer, Sara Blakely, hand-peddled her homemade product into department stores until someone finally took her seriously. Everyone was sold—including Oprah Winfrey, who featured the product on her show and turned the word Spanx into a household name (or at least the female side of the house). There are a few copycat brands, but for a few dollars more the quality of the Spanx product should earn your purchase. Spanx and spanx-like products are a special type of underwear that is worn instead of typical panties. These products are designed to prevent "panty-lines"and smooth out the area from below the bra-line down to the knees, depending on which product you prefer. Spanx type products do not have stays of any kind so there is no chance that they will show through any type of fabric. Spanx and Spanx-type products range in use from simply preventing "lines" to varying amounts of compression. Some products have a built in bra and can be worn as an "all-in-one" type of garment. These products also come with built-in pantyhose if you do not want to show bare legs. Wear these under flowy or clingy gowns—shapely support and no lines!

The PETTICOAT

You don't think you need this, but really, you do! Worn at the natural waist (not on your hips), the petticoat creates fullness in the bottom of your bridal gown. If your gown's skirt is an a-line, princess or ball gown it probably already has some sort of crinoline (crunchy netting) sewn into the lining of the skirt. This is all well and good, but the problem is that because the crinoline is sewn into the dress and is not a separate piece, the netting will not prevent itself from getting caught between your legs while you walk (horrors!). A separate petticoat, sometimes called a crinoline, will keep the underskirt of your dress where it is suppose to be, which is NOT between you legs. Also, by wearing the appropriate fullness petticoat, you will properly show-off the beautiful fabric and shape of the skirt while highlighting the beading. Also, a fuller petticoat can sometimes raise the bottom of the dress eliminating the need for a hem. Petticoats come in various degrees of fullness. A ball gown skirt is meant to be very full. Buy a petticoat that will accommodate the necessary fullness. Play with different sizes of fullness when choosing your wedding dress. One of our brides used a semi-full petticoat when trying on her favorite dress. The dress was "okay" until we put on a fuller petticoat. The fuller skirt created a simple drama that made the dress spectacular! Everyone was crying! Now this was her DREAM dress! Remember, too, that a full bottomed skirt will make your waist look smaller. New mermaid slips are now available and are wonderful at accentuating the curves of a mermaid dress. Sheath-style dresses might not benefit from a petticoat, but from its cousin, the slip. Slips will prevent the dress from being see-through and slips also help prevent your wedding dress from sticking to your legs. The ideal petticoat or slip will have an elastic band around the top or will be ordered according to your waist measurement. Some petticoats can even be ordered with custom lengths in mind for brides that are shorter in stature. Be careful when using a petticoat with a drawstring enclosure, sometimes these can show through.

If you are wearing a full skirted dress and your wedding is going to be in a warmer climate, you might want to investigate a hoop style petticoat. "Hoop skirts", as they are sometimes called, contain flexible plastic "hoops" sewn into the fabric, circling the perimeter of the petticoat. Hoop versions come in different styles with different fullnesses. The fullness is created by the size of the perimeter of the hoops instead of netting. Without netting, your legs will have nothing touching them and will only have openness creating room for air to circulate. Also, the hoops prevent the layers of netting, which although light-weight, from creating bulk and holding in warmth.

My advice is to let your professional consultant help determine which kind of petticoat you will need. Your bridal consultant has seen all kinds of fit both outside and underneath the dresses. You will be amazed at what a difference the right petticoat will make!

DOUBLE-SIDED TAPE.

If you thought that diamonds are a girl's best friend, you would be wrong—it's double-sided tape! Remember that "scandalous" green dress J. Lo wore with the neckline down to her belly button that made fashion history? You know how the neckline kept in place? You got it! Double-sided tape. This fabulous invention is strong but flexible tape that is sticky on both sides. Think Scotch tape on steroids! This tape, sometimes called "fashion tape", will stick fabric to fabric and fabric to skin. Although double-sided tape works miracles, it works best with thinner fabrics. Double-sided tape will not secure a corseted bodice to your skin, nor will it replace a necessary bust alteration. Double-sided tape prevents gaping and keeps off-the-shoulder straps in place. If you are worried that someone can look down your top or that the neck line will open a little, this tape is perfect for keeping the fabric next to the skin. As previously discussed, most bridal fabric is not stretchy. This poses a problem with off-the-shoulder dresses. You cannot keep off- the-shoulder straps in exactly the same place while moving around if the fabric is not stretchy or have some type of elastic in it. Double-sided tape will affix the shoulder straps to exactly where you want the straps to lay across your shoulders. Double-sided tape also has an afterlife. It's great to close gaping button down shirts.

SHOES.

Although shoes are not technically an undergarment, because they are worn under the dress we will discuss it here. Who doesn't LOVE shoes! If you are not a shoe lover, change your view for at least this one occasion. I have seen many brides spend thousands of dollars on her perfect bridal outfit, only to ruin it by throwing on a pair of tennis shoes or flip-flops! Do not believe the statement that I hear all the time: shoes don't matter, the dress will cover them up. Nothing could be further from the truth. If your dress is properly hemmed, it should skim the top of your toes, which is about 1-2 inches off the floor. Do not compare yourself to the bridal models of the runway whose dresses are mere millimeters off the floor. They are professionally trained and are walking on completely flat surfaces. The front tip of your shoe should peek out from under your dress when you walk; if your dress is too long, your toe can catch the hem or under layers of your skirt and you will stumble, or worse, fall. When buying shoes with rhinestones or embellishments, run your fingers across the stones to make sure that the prongs holding the stones are flat and flush. Snags can occur if prong, embellishments or buckles catch the fabric of your skirt.

Wear shoes that fit the formality and décor of your dress. You don't need to be "matchy-matchy" in style, but you should in color. White shoes with an ivory dress look mismatched. Most bridal shoes come in satin, textured satin (called boca), or silk. All but silk can usually be dyed to match your dress, depending on the manufacturer. If you are planning to dye your shoes, MAKE SURE THEY ARE DYEABLE. Just because they are white, does not mean they can be dyed. You cannot believe what kind of shoes walk through our doors with the owner expecting that they can be dyed. No we cannot dye brown leather pumps! A fun trend we are seeing now is the bride wearing blue shoes as her "something blue", or dying them a bold color to match bridesmaids or flowers. Just make sure that they will photograph to compliment your outfit rather than just look like a blaring mistake.

Next, when buying shoes it's important to make sure that they are comfortable. We tell our brides to wear them at home, on carpet, while doing their household chores.

Avoid stiletto heels. Not only are they NOT comfortable, but they can snag the train, put holes in the aisle-runner and get stuck in the grass. Comfortable doesn't mean anything goes. I personally HATE flip-flops. For a lot of reasons. Hearing the soft thump of "flip—flop—flip—flop" padding down the aisle is tacky. It also trivializes the sacredness of your ceremony. Unless you are having a VERY casual ceremony—and by that I mean, the groom is in jeans, and the bride is in a sundress or your actual ceremony is on the sand at the beach, flip-flops are inappropriate. I had a mother of the groom very upset because the bride wanted the groom and all the groomsmen in taupe flip-flops that matched their suits. The wedding was on the beach. The problem (which I agree WAS a problem) was that the beach ceremony was being hosted by a 5 star hotel with a formal reception inside afterwards! We resolved the issue by ordering all the men matching brown shoes to be worn at the reception.

For outdoor weddings there is a wonderful new product called "SoleMates". Sole Mates are flexible clear plastic heel covers that widen the end of the heel so the heel will not push through grass or turf. They are perfect if you don't want to wear a wedge heel. On the internet there is a funny picture of a bridal party where all the women are standing awkwardly because every one of their shoes are stuck deep in the grass. Keep that mental picture in your mind when you are buying shoes for your bridesmaids, and invest in SoleMates!

It is not unusual to wear two different pairs of shoes; one for the wedding, one for the reception. As a true shoe lover, it is my belief that the love of shoes inspired the fun new tradition of wearing a different dress after the wedding for the reception—you would naturally need a different pair of shoes! I'm sure that jewelry lovers, think the same thing about jewelry... If you are wearing different pairs of shoes with the same dress, pay attention to heel heights and have your dress hemmed accordingly. A difference in height can play havoc with your hem; you don't want to be tripping over your dress during your first dance!

Once you have chosen the perfect undergarments and shoes, do NOT forget to bring them to your alteration appointments. My seamstresses will send you back home if you don't have them with you. It is impossible to take in a bust without the bra that you are going to wear. Likewise, it is impossible to pin a hem without wearing the ACTUAL shoes. Don't attempt to say, "well, the shoes are about 2 inches...." Don't let those words escape from your mouth. There is no way that your professional seamstress is going to spend hours pinning, basting, adjusting and sewing a bridal hem using an "approximate" heel height. Pinning the hem involves more than just heel height, your posture when standing in the shoes must be taken in consideration also.

Wow! Who knew that all the things you're not supposed to see could be so important. Actually, no one needs to know. Except your groom, but only if you want him to....

CHAPTER 16

THE PERFECT FIT: TIPS FOR GETTING YOUR DRESS ALTERED

GLORIAJEAN ROSSI

One of the most important things about purchasing the perfect wedding gown is being able to have it fit perfectly. There is much more to alterations than pinning and sewing a seam. There is a big difference between basic tailoring and the skills needed for bridal alterations. Unless your gown has been custom made you will most likely require alterations. A wedding gown that is custom made is sewn according to your exact measurements. Therefore it is critical that you are measured correctly when purchasing your wedding gown. Most bridal salons have experienced bridal consultants that have been trained to correctly measure you. They are knowledgeable of the manufacturers they carry and are familiar with the size chart each company has designed.

All eyes will be on you on your special day and the perfect fit is much more important than the size of the gown that you are wearing. Try not to stress on the number size if it is larger than what you normally wear, you must be aware that traditionally bridal gowns run smaller than your street clothes size. There is not a lot any expert seamstress can do if the dress is too small.

There is also a possibility that your gown can be ordered to the correct length so you won't have to have the gown hemmed. This is called a hollow to hem measurement. In order for this to be done correctly your seamstress does need to be very knowledgeable about this precise measurement. Prior to being measured for a hollow to hem measurement you MUST have the correct shoes, slip and any undergarments that you will be wearing on your special day. I only recommend this when there is no other way to hem the dress because not only do you need the correct measurement from the bridal consultant, you also need to rely on an experienced factory to cut and measure the making of the dress correctly. Miscalculating by just one or two inches can cause you to have to change your shoes or slip and you may not end up having the look you dreamed of.

You can also end up purchasing your dress from a salon that sells right off the rack. This will allow you to see the fit of the dress you chose to your size with minimal adjustments for that perfect fit. If the salon does not have a seamstress on staff they will have bridal consultants that are experienced in knowing what lines on the dress need to be in place for you to have a great fit. They will be able to help you with knowing what custom changes can be done by an experienced seamstress and what cannot be changed. It is very important that you are knowledgeable about what can and cannot be altered before you purchase your dress because there is nothing more devastating then being told by the seamstress after the purchase that it can't be fixed.

The most important thing on the fit of the gown is the placement of the bust seams. If you are smaller busted the seams can sometime fall too far to the sides. Women with larger busts can find that alterations place the bust seams too close to the middle. The bust seams can be moved but if at all possible that would be the last place I would recommend adjusting.

Depending on the details on your gown one of the easiest adjustments can be taking the sides in. In many cases the stress of handling all the details of planning a wedding equates to the bride to be losing a few pounds and even a loss of five pounds may require an adjustment to your gown for a proper fit. It is essential that you have confidence in the ability and knowledge of your seamstress. Don't be afraid to ask for referrals if you have to use an off site seamstress.

You may find that you have fallen in love with 75% of the gown but that there is something missing or that you are not sure of. Possibly the addition of a cap sleeve, a little more appliqué, extra hem lace or the removal of a flower, waistband, or too much crinoline can turn this dress into your perfect dream gown. An expert seamstress will be able to let you know what can and cannot be done to your dress without ruining the original look of the gown. Many times just removing a layer of crinoline from the skirt of the gown will make the gown lay softer.

The majority of wedding gowns today are strapless and a perfect fit is necessary so you will feel secure in the gown throughout your day. An expert seamstress will know that fitting the gown to the ribcage perfectly will feel better than fitting the bust tightly to keep the dress up. When the bust is fitted too tightly your skin will bulge over and look unattractive in your pictures, or you will tug at the gown all day. Fitting the ribcage tightly and bust slightly looser allows you to fall into the dress so there isn't any bulge and prevents the need to tug at your dress.

If your perfect gown is an exquisite gown with a beautiful cap sleeve it is important that the sleeves be attached in the proper place. Cap sleeves that are placed too far to the side will leave you feeling that they are going to fall off your shoulders. Properly attached in front and back they will allow you to move quite freely without feeling that they will slide off. You should not have to use two sided tape to keep it on your shoulder.

The sides of the gown should be fitted to follow the contour of your body cutting under your bust for good definition. The gown should flow to the waist with a slimming appearance continuing over the hip for that hourglass shape, unless you have chosen a natural waisted gown. The gown should cut under the bust to a shapely waist usually having a band at the waist and a ball skirt covering the hip.

Having a good repoire with the seamstress is very important so she/ he will fit your dress the way you personally feel comfortable in. A lot of times girls are self consciencous of their hips so when you're wearing a fit and flare gown the seamstress should fit you a little less snuggly in the hip area so you feel comfortable. Some brides are okay with their hips and want it fitted tightly. Make sure you are comfortable with the alterations being done.

Some seamstresses are very good at sewing gowns from patterns and others are great at altering a gown to fit a body. Don't ever be shy to ask for referrals or even look at some pictures of brides that she/he has fitted before. I know I myself cringe when I open the newspaper and see pictures of brides in strapless gowns and their skin is bulging over the gown. Always ask how much experience your seamstress has in altering wedding gowns in terms of years of experience.

The next part of the alterations on your gown and a very important part is the bustle since that is the way the gown is worn for the majority of the reception. Bustling is generally done after the wedding ceremony and pictures to allow the bride more freedom of movement without dragging the train. Since all brides are not the same height your bustle should be custom made. Your bustle should lift the back of your gown to your hem length.

There are several different types of bustles. A traditional or over bustle is when the train of the gown is pulled up and attached to the top layer of the dress. The determination of where the train is attached is dependent on the style of the skirt. A ball or full skirt is almost always attached at the waist. A slim aline, mermaid,or a fit and flare gown is either attached at the knee or mid thigh point depending on the length and shape of the train. Gowns with pick up skirts have to be bustled to follow the basic pattern of the pick ups.

The points where the attachments are made for the specific bustle can be either with a hook and eye or a clear flat button and a crocheted thread loop. The hook and eye should be used as a last resort because it easily unhooks itself when the bride moves, sits or dances even though it's the easiest and most inexpensive to do. The button and loop is much more secure especially when using the flat clear button. It's very strong for the very heavy gowns that are so popular today. A covered button should not be used even though they are more attractive because the heads of the button pop off when the loop is placed and removed too often. The seamstress should also make two crocheted loops on the main point so if one loop should break there is a backup to use.

The second most popular bustle is a French bustle. This isn't the best choice for every dress. The skirt needs to be fuller and a slightly longer train to get the proper look. This bustle is done the best with ribbons. The ribbons can be either tied to each other or they can be tied to buttons or pulled through loops. With this type of bustle it is important that the attendant that is responsible for assisting the bride is taught this technique.

Another type is an under bustle. This type should be used for brides who don't like bustles or on gowns with embellishments on the upper part of the back of the skirt and plain hemline. The bustling is done with ribbons and basically looks like there isn't a train because it is secured to the underneath of the dress with the ribbons.

There are a lot of other ways to pull up the train on your wedding gown and an experienced bridal gown seamstress will be able to advise you on the best type for your dress.

CHAPTER 17

GETTING GORGEOUS: HAIR AND MAKEUP TIPS FOR YOUR BIG DAY

RACHEL ESPOSITO

When it comes to your big day, hair and makeup arguably play one of the biggest parts in that little girl fantasy some of us have. We all want to look like the perfect bride, like one any prince would be unable to resist. You should be in the planning stage already, and planning your hair and makeup might just be one of the most important things of all to consider, especially when it comes to the wedding pictures. Planning your overall look well in advance is key to creating beautiful photos and memories, and with the help and advice from professionals, you can be assured to achieve the style and look you have always dreamed of.

It is very important that your makeup and hair matches your wedding dress, as well as the overall color scheme of the wedding. You do not want to look back at your wedding photos and video and realize that there was any form of color or style conflicts. Whether you have, or are still on the lookout for the perfect wedding dress, your hair and makeup should most surely match its beautiful design. This is why it is very important to choose your gown early in the planning process, after you have chosen your venue.

We all see the fashion articles in magazines, some of which include bridal guides packed with appealing pictures of models with perfect hair and makeup. These magazines can be useful, make no mistake, but please understand that this is pure advertising and the fact is those specific pictures' makeup or hairstyle won't necessarily flatter an average woman. In this chapter I will share some valuable information with you before you decide on what makeup to buy, or how to style your hair for this very special event.

Starting with makeup, it is vital that you understand your skin type, and which products will produce the best results. Here you will find information on various skin types, each with its own pros and cons, and how to avoid the negatives. The skin type, product and color will play a major part in what will look best for you, and it is of utmost importance that you prepare your skin in advance as best as possible in order to have the perfect makeup on your special day.

When it comes to your skin, and what makeup to wear, a few things should be considered, for example, do you have:

- Oily or dry skin

- Normal or sensitive skin

- Combination skin

- Light or dark complexion

It is essential that you take proper care of your skin in the days leading up to your wedding day, should you want your makeup to look absolutely perfect when it needs to. Below I have listed a few general tips on caring for your skin ahead of your big day, ensuring that your makeup looks stunning when all the cameras are upon you, along with which type of products to avoid or to be on the lookout for.

Oily Skin:

If you have oily skin, most makeup brands tend to 'disappear' after a few hours going about your everyday life, and therefore it is critical that you do your research on what makeup works and how to avoid this from happening on the most important day of your life. If you are reading this, no need to worry about where to do this research, as we have already done this for you.

Oily skin tends to look shiny or greasy, which is mainly caused by large open pores and could result in acne in most cases, and is also very prone to blemishes and blackheads. This skin type could be quite problematic in general and especially when it comes to makeup for your wedding day, unless of course, you know which steps to follow.

Regular cleaning is a must for this skin type, as it builds up a lot of dirt due to the oily surface of the skin. Luckily there are numerous cleaning products on the market for oily skin, as many people have this in common. A good facial scrub works best to lift the dirt and leave the skin fresh. Many of these products also block the pores, decreasing oil production of the skin, but this is not always good as it can also trap the dirt, causing acne. The best advice I can give is to always go for the well-known and trusted names in the skincare industry, as they were built on success.

Foods that are high in carbohydrates also increase the amount of oil your skin produces, and thus it is vital that you minimize the intake of such foods for a few weeks, or even months before your wedding day. These foods include certain fruits, sweets, soft drinks, pastas, potatoes, bran (also found in some cereals), bread, rice and beans. Not all of these are equally bad; however, especially avoid sweets, chocolates and soft drinks as they are your enemy!

Make sure that whichever facial cream you use is well suited to your skin, as many creams could worsen the situation should you choose an incompatible product. Even if your facial cream seems to work for you, try and minimize the application of creams before the big day just to be on the safe side. The avoidance of facial creams can, in many cases, drastically improve the quality of your skin, regardless of what the media tells you. Seek out products that indicate features like "Sweat Proof" or "Oil Free" as these will be your best options, and try to avoid anything that is not oil free.

There is a good side to having oily skin though, as this skin type is less likely to produce wrinkles at an early age, something we all dread. Your skin will generally age significantly slower with proper and correct care. When it comes to makeup, it is recommended to invest in a good foundation primer, as it will minimize the appearance of pores and provide a good foundation for your main base. Using a base that has a mineral foundation will be of great benefit to your skin as it will drain any excess oil from your skin which is caused by the sebaceous, or oil glands, producing more oil than your skin actually needs, and is the main reason behind oily skin. Mascara tends to run off or disappear on oily skin surfaces, and you should thus use a powder foundation underneath to avoid having this problem as powders add some protection for oily surfaces.

Dry Skin:

Dry skin could also prove to be quite a bit of a problem when it comes to makeup. This can be caused by various factors including changes in weather, for example: wind tends to dry out the skin and dry skin is also very common during the colder months as the air itself can dry out the skin. It could also be that, like the opposite of oily skins, the pores are a bit smaller and do not produce sufficient oil to moisturize the skin properly, resulting in skin that is left feeling tight, dry, and flaky after washing your face and wiping it dry. This could prove to be quite the nightmare when applying a base coat to your face, as it will make the flakes more visible, and this is most definitely not what you want to occur on your wedding day pictures.

This skin type is known to develop red patches, wrinkles, an unnaturally pale and yellowish tone or complexion, and is extremely prone to aging and skin irritations. There are quite a few tips and tricks to help with dry skin, and you can keep it looking healthy with regular application of natural facial masks, moisturizers, beauty treatments, or even just regular skincare products that have some form of moisturizing ingredient. Once again, here it is best to stick with the more well known brands on the market, as some less-expensive products may worsen the situation.

Be on the lookout for skincare products or facial creams containing natural hypoallergenic ingredients as these ingredients are very good at moisturizing for beautiful, healthy looking skin. Some skincare companies or brands sometimes use the phrase, "contains mineral oils" on the actual packaging or on their advertising campaigns. Do not be fooled though, as mineral oils aren't always a good option when it comes to dry skin, and should mostly be avoided. Your best option is to lean towards natural creams, which are rich in healthy moisturizing components and could prove to be a life saver before such a big event. Natural lotions and creams also have great healing capabilities, and prevent skin from aging at a fast and unnatural rate. Most of these creams are also great for dry or chapped lips, and after researching many opinions from everyday people, proved to be even better than the usual "anti-dry lips" products!

Try them! Natural products should have no side effects whatsoever and should be safe to apply to your lips, this is a great tip for those who have not yet discovered this, as their ingredients' main quality is to heal and deeply moisturize any skin surface. More fantastic advice, straight from the mouths of numerous qualified dermatologists, is to limit the amount of time you spend in the bath or shower, as your skin absorbs water at quite a fast rate. How could water be bad for dry skin? Remember, the water that runs from your tap is not pure and healthy, and contains numerous harmful chemicals produced during the water refining stages: these chemicals could do much damage to your skin. It is widely suggested to spend no more than three to five minutes in the bath or shower, and to use a very gentle soap for your face. Soaps that are colored (blue, green, pink, yellow) should also be avoided, as the colorants in these are slightly more harmful than the ones found in soaps of a white color. After your shower, or washing your face, gently pat the skin dry with a towel and avoid rubbing or scrubbing the face dry, as this will make the dry flakes more visible.

When it comes to toners, try to use cosmetic milk products, creams, lotions, or any product that states "100% natural", make sure that they are alcohol free, as alcohol dries the skin out even more and should be avoided at all times. Products containing alcohol can also cause irritation of the skin and in many cases worsen the overall appearance of your skin, and since you will have tons of pictures taken on the big day, this is the last thing you want.

Cosmetic milk products and/or toners are very effective when it comes to purifying and refining facial pores, aiding in the rehydration of the skin and leave it feeling much smoother and softer than before.

Normal Skin:
Known to be the least problematic of all skin types, normal skin looks and feels healthy, elastic and supple. Even though your skin might look smooth, feel soft, and rarely give you any real problems, the stress of planning a wedding can be disastrous for even the healthiest looking skin. Stress is known to cause various skin problems, and as you surely know, planning a wedding is a stressful time, and the stress will continue to increase as the big day draws closer and closer. It is therefore vital that you do not ignore spending some quality time on your already natural, good looking skin. The skin tissue of normal skin will not visibly show any trace of oil, but this does not mean that your skin is oil-free. Your

skin provides good circulation thanks to medium-sized pores, giving you a natural and healthy complexion.

 Even though this specific skin type requires minimal maintenance, you need to keep a close eye on your skin as the wedding draws near. Should you discover any difference in your skin, be sure to try a different facial soap with natural moisturizers to improve any skin outbreaks before it becomes a problem. See the "Oily Skin" and "Dry Skin" in the previous sections depending on your situation, as different skin types react differently to stress-related skin problems. The best advice here is to stick with what you are already using, if you don't see any changes. If you do see a change at any stage, simply avoid products with too many chemicals or colorants, and try a simple white moisturizing soap that is gentle on the skin.

Normal skin can be a real blessing, and will leave your skin looking good for years to come. Just make sure it is as perfect on your wedding day when the entire spotlight will be on you!

Sensitive Skin:
The range of products on the market that is designed for sensitive skin is endless. The skin surface tends to be very dry and quite irritable, making finding the right product to match your skin type extremely difficult. With so many products out there it is hard to determine what works, and what is simply false advertising. Because sensitive skin typically develops reddish spots on your face that could become itchy or scaly if proper care is not taken, it is vital that you do proper product research before buying every "sensitive skin" product out there.

Your skin feels tight, easily becomes inflamed and can break into spots at any moment, thus it is important to keep makeup to a minimum even when you have a trusted product. Just because the product works for a million others does not mean it will work for you. Sensitive skin has various stages, some are quite simply more irritated by chemicals than others, and has its own unique features and reactions to certain ingredients used in makeup products.

When it comes to makeup, your best bet would be to try and stay away from any liquid makeup products such as base. Rather than using a liquid base, use powder-based products as these normally have remarkably less ingredients that might trigger a much unwanted skin irritation. For those who prefer not to use powder makeup when it comes to the base or foundation, it is highly recommended to keep a lookout for silicone-based foundations, as they produce noticeably less skin irritation and problems than other liquid foundations.

It has also been noted by dermatologists that when it comes to eye- and lip liners, it is best to stick with black, as this is the color least likely to cause an irritation of the skin. It is also recommended to once again stick with pencils rather than any form of liquid eyeliners. We know that this will be a very happy and emotional day in your life, but please avoid waterproof makeup, as these generally have added chemicals that can cause an outbreak on your skin when you least want it, then there won't only be tears of happiness.

When using blushes, stick to natural colors such as cream, beige, white, or any light color. As with soaps, the colorant used in these products can cause quite a few problems, especially with sensitive skin, so take extra care.

Combination Skin:
Probably one of the most common skin types found in most women, combination skin can be identified by dry or normal, smooth cheeks, with an oily forehead, nose, and chin area, commonly known as the "T-Zone". This is a good type of skin, as with the correct and proper care you can prolong your youth a bit and wrinkles will only start to show in later years.

You will need different products for the different skin areas and surfaces if you want a nice and even tone or complexion. The dry zones around the cheek area should be treated with natural moisturizers as these are rich in protein for the skin. Avoid using any product that has a mineral base, as these products will dry out the skin even further. While on the other end of course, when treating the T-zone of the face which is oily, mineral-based products are encouraged just for the fact that it can help keep oil production by the skin under control. Clean your face regularly (at least twice a day) as the so-called T-zone can build up a lot of dirt throughout the day.

This type of skin generally has good circulation, but your skin sometimes tends to get dry, while spots could break out at any time. This is not uncommon in combination skin as pimples will usually appear in the T-zone of your face. Your only problem here is the oily parts where pimples seem to appear, as the dry parts can easily be taken care of by a wide range of natural moisturizing products available on the market today. Just be sure to not to confuse 'natural' products with 'mineral' products, as mineral products can be very harmful to dry skin and cause it to dry out even further, but these are a blessing to the oily areas as it keeps your skins' oil production under firm control once you have the right product.

Pimples form due to everyday dirt that gets stuck to the oily surface of the skin and block the pores. This can even cause infections and blemishes in some cases. The best way to prepare your skin before applying that extra important makeup on the day, is to wash your face at least twice a day with any facial soap with plant extracts, as this will nourish the skin while the minerals will reduce oil production with regular use.

Using natural toners is always a fantastic idea, and for combination skin a toner with plant and mineral extracts works best in most cases, as it helps in the removal of any excess oil and dirt on the skin surface.

The complexion of your skin:
A darker complexion skin will generally compliment colors much better compared to lighter skin, and therefore you can push your normal limits on the colors you would usually use and do some experimenting. Dark colors tend to look bright, and sometimes quite exotic, for example dark blue or green eye shadow, or dark red lipstick. This type of skin is

more vulnerable to sunrays though, although not usually as visible as on lighter skins, but proper care should be taken when heading outdoors by using a foundation with an SPF ingredient, that offers protection against UV-rays.

For lighter complexions it is always advisable to stick to a natural cream, beige, white, or tan base. If your makeup base can be applied with your fingers instead of a sponge (i.e. liquid foundations), it is highly recommended to give it a try, as you will be able to even the color out much more evenly and faster than with a sponge. It is critical that you avoid having that makeup line around the frame of your face by choosing a foundation that matches your skin 100%.

When you are in a shop looking for a new makeup base and you are not sure about what you have chosen, but the color is very close to that of your skin, ask a store assistant for advice before rushing to the counter! These associates are well trained and most of them are formally trained and have been doing makeovers on their family and friends since a very early age so they can offer great advice. This line around the face will be slightly more visible on lighter skin types, other than that, go for soft, natural colors when choosing makeup. This will look elegant and fairy-like.

General Makeup Tips

Lips are something we haven't spoken too much about in this chapter so far, so let's start there.

Whatever your skin type or color, it is advisable to make use of pink lipstick, or a shade thereof. This will not only give you that soft, sexy, feminine look, but will also look great on your wedding photos, as the flash of a camera compliments pink tones very well. Although the more glossy type lipsticks on the market are not for everyone, it is highly fashionable in our day and age, and if you find the right color you might just love it.

Whichever color you decide on when choosing a lipstick, make sure it is at least a shade or two brighter than your natural lip color, to ensure that perfect smile. Lip liners of a slightly darker color than your lipstick can make your lips look even fuller and will make the overall look last longer. Thus ensuring you have gorgeous looking lips until the end of your day.

If your skin itself shows any kind of redness, apply a light foundation to even it out by using your fingertips. Try and use a foundation that has a slight yellowish tone, as this will also look good on the pictures afterwards.

One of the biggest worries most women have when it comes to makeup on their wedding day, is the fear that their eyeliner might smudge or smear. Make no mistake, this is going to be an emotional day, even if you don't plan on crying, the combination of happiness and excitement can do strange things to a person. You should consider buying water-resistant eyeliner that won't ruin your perfect makeup because of a few tears of happiness and excitement. On this day water resistant mascaras are always encouraged, unless of course you have sensitive skin that will be irritated by this type of mascara. You can gently apply a highlighter shade to the brow bone, while trying to match your eye color, which will make your eyes stand out and look alive. Be sure not to cross the corners of the eyebrows as this will look unnatural, unless you have a specific style in mind that requires this of course.

If it is a beautiful, natural, yet striking appearance you are after, use two shades of blush. Apply the lighter shade to the apples of your cheeks first, then gently rub upwards toward your hairline and soften it up with few downward touches. Next you apply the darker shade, but only on the cheekbones, as this will give a great dimension to your face and the overall look of your makeup and appearance.

Remember to always bring a backup makeup emergency kit along on your wedding day, ensure that you have a small bag to match your wedding dress which could be used to keep the essential items close to you at all times, just in case. You want the makeup products in your bag to be trusted and the only way to know this is to only carry products on you that you have tried before, as this is most surely not the best day to find out that you are allergic to a certain item you grabbed off the shelf without ever testing it on your skin. In this bag should only be products that you know, and know well.

The biggest secret: never wear too much make up, lean towards softer colors, and make sure these colors fit with your wedding's overall color scheme. A qualified skin-care associate could also provide excellent advice and can be found in nearly any shop that sells a wide range of makeup and skincare products.

Hair Tips

When choosing a hairstyle, you should always try to compliment your wedding dress according to the style or formality. To ensure that you have strong, shiny looking hair, it is also suggested by some leading experts in the hair industry to consume foods rich in vitamin B12, such as avocado or foods made with olive oil. These will feed your hair and help strengthen them in time for the wedding.

A worry for some future brides with shorter hair is the drama of deciding on which hairstyle to choose, since the options could seem so limited. This could be no further from the truth, as there are numerous hairstyles available today if you keep an eye out for them, even when walking around in a mall while shopping (which you will most likely do much of). On the other hand, sometimes keeping it simple can look best. Maybe a slightly 'upgraded' version of what you already have, meaning healthier and shinier. But we will get to that in a moment. A simple look, especially with short hair can look very sexy and elegant indeed, and that is exactly what you might be looking for.

With long hair it simply comes down to breakage, as this could be easily spotted on the high resolution photos that a wedding photographer or any quality camera with a bright flash will produce. Sure, there are other things to keep in mind such as how healthy and exquisite your hair looks as it blows in the wind, but finding a solution for damaged and/ or broken hair should be your first step. The fact is that damaged hair could potentially take up to six months to be restored back to its proper, healthy state. The hair industry literally has tons of products on the market to help you in this. Always go for trusted names, even though they are sometimes remarkably more expensive, this is supposed to be the best day of your life so you want to look the best you possibly can!

Everything from creams, shampoos, conditioners, and all different forms of hair moisturizers and repair products are available almost everywhere. This is important. Another tip worth mentioning is not to wash your hair on your wedding day as your hair takes roughly 24 hours to settle after a wash, and will look at its best at that time. Hair salons or studios could also offer valuable advice when it comes to hair products, so it's always a great place to turn to if you have no idea what products to start with.

If you have long hair, finding a hairstyle should not be too much of a problem for you. The internet is loaded with ideas and you have so many options available to you. The best thing you can do is to buy bridal magazines or visit your local hair studio to get an idea of what style to go for and what would suit you best, that is if you have not had that perfect style already in mind since your childhood.

Should you be looking for something simple, the first question would be whether you want your hair curly or straight, as 'simple' takes an upward hairstyle out of the question, even though there are some simple upward hairstyles, they aren't always too easy to get perfect. A straight forward downward style is recommended, unless you want your hair to have added elegance to fit with the rest of your attire. Big curls are extremely sexy, have been in fashion for many years, and are still going strong. You cannot go wrong here, especially if your hair is longer than average.

Straight hair has always been a winner too, we see it in all magazines and television shows, and some women always talk about how much they want straight hair. This speaks for itself. When it comes to simple, straight hair would be the ultimate answer. If you do not have naturally straight hair, but dream of walking down the aisle with beautiful, silky smooth straight hair,  avoid using any hair straightening product that uses extreme heat that will damage your hair beyond repair. To simply blow dry your hair (or done by the hairdresser) using a low heat setting works just as well, and will do significantly less damage to your hair.

Your best friend for beautiful hair would be the experts, love them or hate them; hair salons know a lot more about hair than the average person, especially when it comes to bridal styles. Even if you don't buy the products they will show to you, you could definitely pick up a few good pointers on how to get your hair ready in time. It is normal (and recommended) to go for at least three sessions at your hairdresser before your big day, as they will use proper hair treatments that are known to work and will take care of 95% of the flaws your hair might have, ensuring that your hair looks at its absolute best. This could be costly, but this is the one time in your life where you are allowed to reach a bit deeper into your purse. You deserve the best after all. You can experiment with different styles before deciding on the final style with your local hairdresser, and if your dress comes with a veil or head piece, they could surely arrange your style accordingly. Just make sure the hair stylist knows exactly what you want!

Your hair stylist should be very open about their intentions for your hair, and if they seem to be too quiet, do not be afraid to ask them what they are doing. Sometimes they tend to let their own childhood fantasies about being a bride get in the way. We have all walked away from a hairdresser disappointed at some stage in our lives, and needless to say, this is surely the last thing you want to happen on the day of your wedding. In addition, don't be afraid to try several different stylists before settling on one. Researching your hair stylist should begin after you have chosen your gown and settled on the "look" you would like for your big day.

Adding hair pieces or extensions is also something to consider if you want to give your hair an extra dimension or special overall look. Extensions can add length and even volume to your hair should you need or desire so. It could also come very handy when you know that you are getting married during a windy month, and your hair is not quite heavy enough to keep itself down if the wind decides to rise (This is especially useful for outside and beach weddings as it will add some extra weight to your hair to keep it from blowing in all directions.).

A lot of us color our hair to look even and perfect, or to hide grey or dull areas. It is advisable to color your hair twice before the wedding; the second time should be no closer than two weeks before the wedding. The use of hair colorants damage your hair, regardless of what the box or the inside pamphlet might say. Thus, you should invest more time in conditioning and moisturizing your hair with products designed for colored hair to restore your hair's natural beauty as quickly as possible.

Go for a style that works, and has looked pretty on others that have been married before you. Do not try anything too extravagant, unless it is extremely well planned in advance. The last thing you want is for people to talk about a ridiculous hairstyle, yours. Simple is almost always best.

The big day: Hair and Makeup Checklist
Remember your emergency cosmetics case, which should be carried close to you in case of emergency. This should include:

- Eye drops, as crying will give you red eyes that never look too glamorous on wedding photos.

- A concealer with a small application wand for quick touch-ups

- A powder-based foundation to touch up on any shiny areas of the skin due to perspiration and to avoid having skin that might look too shiny on the pictures, if you have generally oily skin, rather carry oil blotching pads instead of applying more foundation as this could lead to disaster

- Lip liner, gloss and lipstick for a quick fix if needed

- Makeup removal pen, just in case your makeup smears and you need to re-apply to some areas, which will make it much quicker and not noticeable if you sneak away to the restrooms for a touchup.

When it comes to your lips, having a long lasting color that stays is the prime concern. A quick tip from leading makeup experts that consults with many celebrities, recommends:

- The first step to achieving long lasting lip color is to first apply a primer to the lips which will lock in the color pigments of your lips and make them look more alive.

- Next, when choosing your lipstick, always be on the lookout for "long lasting" or "all day" lipsticks as this will surely aid in having perfect lips.

- Third, use a natural gloss to add some shine and compliment the actual color of your lipstick. Clear lip gloss works best to add a healthy, sexy shine. Lips that have these three layers can last twice as long as lips with a single lipstick layer. Remember this, and don't forget to use lip liner to bring out the fullness of your smile.

- Lipstick tends to look brighter on photos, so avoid colors that appear too bright, but also stay away from colors that are lighter than your actual lip color.

For perfect looking skin at the wedding, it is vital that you get a good night's rest before the actual wedding day to avoid your skin looking tired on the pictures. Here are some more tips for when the big day arrives:

- Even though every bride wants to look flashy, it is best to avoid products with shimmer, especially when it comes to your foundation. A matte foundation always looks best. If you want an added shimmer, apply a small amount to the cheekbones only.

- Applying a primer foundation will also increase the longevity of your makeup, and should be applied with a foundation brush that will give you a soft, airbrushed look.

- When applying the main foundation, a good brand of moisturizing foundation will look best in the photos, and decrease the chance of having that dreaded line around the face. Even it out by using your fingertips, as this will give you a bit more control with most foundations.

- Choosing an all purpose concealer with multiple shades works best to hide any redness or imperfections, so have this at hand just in case you might need it.

- Stick to natural shades when applying blush, and use two coats as explained in the "general makeup tips"section, and only use colors that you know look great on your skin.

- When using a foundation with SPF for sun protection, limit the amount you apply as this ingredient might give a white shine that you do not want.

- When applying blush, lean towards a light pink shade for lighter skin, and plum for darker skin types. These will compliment your tones.

For your eyes, it is best to lean more towards soft, natural colors that match the rest of your attire. Most importantly, if possible, use waterproof mascaras, as this could be a lifesaver!

- Increase the amount of eyeliner you would normally use, but try and avoid black eyeliner and replace it with something more neutral to your skin as black may look a bit stark sometimes.

· Line your eyes as close as possible to the lash line to ensure the most natural definition.

· When applying eye shadow, it will be best to choose a neutral matte or semi-matte shade that would make the eyes pop out a bit better, and don't be scared to use a product with a slight shimmer on the brow bone to compliment your natural look.

· Never forget the eyebrows, and make sure to fill them with a powder brow color that matches the color of your hair. Also be careful not to thin out the brow hairline too much by plucking.

Your hair should not be washed on your wedding day, as much as you want your hair to look healthy, this is not the way to do it. Wash your hair 24 hours before the wedding day to give it time to settle, this is when it will look at its best.

· Small flowers, a veil and accessories are recommended (but not a must) for that fairy tale looking hair you have always wanted. Not only will this add an extra feminine touch but also add some spice to your overall look and will make those wedding memories a bit more special when looking back.

· It is not always the best option to have a friend or family member help in this department, regardless of how important they are to you. Always seek help from a professional, therefore if you aren't happy with what they have done, it can be fixed in record time and you don't have to worry about hurting anybody's feelings.

· The biggest tip here is to simply care for your hair before the wedding day with natural hair treatments, and to have a clear vision and plan of what you want your hair to look like. Here the experts are your best friends in helping you look like the fabulous bride that you are meant to be!

CHAPTER 18

DRESSING THE GROOM: MEN'S FASHION TIPS

SHANNON LINDQUIST

Brides spend a great deal of time searching for the perfect wedding gown, and great dresses for all the ladies in the wedding party. The groom and men of the wedding deserve to look and feel just as stylish and fashion forward as the women. Many changes in wedding planning have come about in recent years; the groom getting involved with picking out formalwear is one big change. Brides are typically delighted to hear that the groom wants to participate in the selection of the men's attire.

There are some traditional rules as far as what to wear for weddings during the day versus at night that people have felt inclined to follow in the past, but in recent years the new state of mind about the planning of weddings has lead people away from these rules and into the thinking that it is their wedding and what they want to do is what they should do instead of following the rules.

The first thing to consider when picking out attire for the men in your wedding is the style or theme of your wedding day. Will your day be formal, informal, colorful, classic, trendy, or modern? The style of your wedding will play an important role in what you choose for your men's formalwear. If your style is simple and informal or if you are having a beach wedding, choosing a suit for a more relaxed and informal look may be a good way to go. You may also choose a three piece option with pants or shorts, a shirt and tie to achieve a casual, laid-back look. If you're planning a day that will be traditional and formal, you may choose to wear a full tuxedo complete with a vest or cummerbund and tie. If your look is trendy and modern, you may choose to skip the vest and go for the tie only look. Once you choose which pieces you wish for all the men to wear then you can start to think about color.

After you decide on the style of your wedding, you'll need to determine the colors the men will wear. This not only includes the color of the vest, tie and pocket square, but the color of the tuxedo itself. You will have plenty of options with the many tuxedo colors available. The most traditional color for tuxedos is basic black. If you are going away from the classic look on your big day there are a number other colors to choose from; chocolate brown, khaki, light or dark gray and navy blue are some great choices if you want a darker color but are trying to get away from black. There are also white and ivory tuxes, many times only the groom will wear one of these to match the bride and the rest of the wedding party will wear a different darker colored tux or suit. You can get very creative with the coordination of your vest, tie and pocket square. Mix and match patterns and colors that compliment each other for added variation and interest. If you've chosen a two tone bridesmaid dress, you can mix your vest and tie or tie and pocket square with the two different colors for the perfect compliment.

The jacket is a very important piece to your tuxedo look. This decision can sometimes be overwhelming, but it is nice to have options! There are many different factors which you should consider when picking out the jacket for your tuxedos, the build of the groom and wedding party should be one major factor on which you base your decision. If the majority of the men in your wedding are tall and slim they will look great in many different styles, one look that slim men can pull off that many others cannot is a longer jacket with four or five buttons. For guys who are a bit broader a jacket with a shawl collar which is rounded off and smooth with little detail and one or two buttons that cuts in at the waist will elongate the body. Another thing to keep in mind when thinking about finding formalwear for larger men is that black is very slimming. The peak lapel is a classic look along with the notch lapel. These jackets usually have a deep v which can be very flattering for all body types. Variation is created with subtle details such as tone on tone satin bands, chalk striping, pin striping, and tone on tone texture.

The trousers for the tuxedo jacket will be determined, somewhat, by the jacket you've selected. If the jacket you've selected has a pattern or details in it there is, more than likely, a matching trouser to go with it. If you've chosen a solid jacket without pattern, you can usually choose from a flat front or pleated trouser for your wedding party. The front of the trousers is where you will see the difference between pleated and flat front as they are just as their names say flat in the front or pleated. The side of the trouser will typically have a satin stripe down the side of it on both legs. You should take into consideration the overall size of your wedding party. If your men are more on the athletic side, you could sport a flat front tuxedo. If your men are not very fit and need a little room in their trousers, a better choice would be a pleated trouser for your group. In general, the same style and color trousers should be worn throughout the men in the wedding party.

Shirts provide another opportunity to add character to your wedding day attire. There are several different shirt styles to choose from. The collar is the most noticeable detail of the shirt that you will have a chance to pick out, there are lay down, banded, and wing-tip collars. When you are choosing which sort of collar you will want it is important to keep in mind what style of tie you will want the men to wear. A lay down collar will normally accommodate any style of tie, while a banded collar is typically worn with no tie. The wing tip collar looks best with a classic bow tie or string tie. Pleating is also added to some styles of cotton shirts to give a traditional look. The basic colors for shirts are white and ivory, which should be based off the brides wedding dress. You can also choose colored shirts such as pink, blue, black or chocolate, some of which may also have a whisper stripe. Microfiber material is the latest most popular material today providing a very smooth texture and feel and often many color options.

Accessories put the finishing touches on your whole wedding day look. The vest or cummerbund, tie, pocket square, studs and cuff links, and shoes not only bring your whole look together but are also another great way to reflect your own personal style.

Vests and cummerbunds can drastically alter the look of your tux. In the past a cummerbund was a staple for all tuxedos. Recently, vests have become all the rage as they seem to be a more flattering way to add color to your tux (or just keep the guys looking great when they decide to take off their jackets). Vests come in many different colors and textures and there are even camouflage and tropical prints to choose from. You may choose to have the men in your wedding wear neither a vest nor cummerbund if you are going for a more casual look.

In many cases the groom chooses the white or ivory accessories. The vest, tie and pocket square should match the color of the bridal gown if you decide to go with white or ivory. The groomsmen typically go in the color of the bridesmaid's dresses, but the same pattern as the groom. The ushers of the wedding can vary with an accent color or a neutral color, such as silver. The fathers of the wedding should have a neutral color, like black, to be easily paired up with the moms of the wedding. The patterns and style can all be the same, but the colors can vary according to the role of the person in the wedding.

Ties come in many different styles, patterns, and colors. The different tie styles can really change the look of your formalwear. Bow ties are typically a more classic and formal look and are often a solid color or black but some of them do come in a textured or patterned fabric. The Windsor tie has become increasingly more popular in recent years; it creates a more modern and slightly more casual look than the bow tie. Windsor ties come in a wide array of patterns, textures, and colors. Some other less common ties that can create very unique looks are the cravat, string, bolo, and cross over ties. The cravat is usually tied in an ascot knot and is a vintage look usually paired with a cut away jacket. The string, crossover, and bolo ties are perfect for a western themed wedding as they look great when paired with a dark jean and casual jacket.

Pocket squares are a great way to add a splash of color to your tuxedo jacket; they come in many different colors and patterns. Many people match the pocket square with the tie they have chosen, or choose a completely different accent color. Pocket squares can also be folded in different ways; folding techniques range from basic to exotic. Some of the more popular folds are the winged puff, three fold stairs, and the four point crown. Any way you fold a pocket square, you will add a little bit of personal flair and color.

Cufflinks and studs give your shirt a very polished look. The selection of cuff links vary greatly from a simple black and silver to a show stopping diamond studded accent or a personalized link with an engraved monogram. Again, the style of your wedding should be kept in mind when picking out all accessories.

Shoes should be the last thing that you pick out, once you have the rest of the tux all figured out then you can choose a pair of shoes that will match. The classic shiny black tux shoe is the most commonly chosen option; there is also a shiny black shoe with a square toe that is becoming popular. There are many other ways you can go with your shoe selection, there are matte shoes in black and brown, usually these look best with a more casual look such as, a suit, in the corresponding color. If the color you have chosen for your tuxedos is white or ivory then a shiny white or ivory shoe would look best. There are even shiny black sneakers made as a tux shoe for the man who can't live a day with out the comfort of tennis shoes. These days people are getting very creative allowing their groomsmen to wear actual tennis shoes or other matching shoes. In some western themed weddings a cowboy boot is appropriate.

No matter what you choose for all of the men in your wedding to wear try to take into consideration what they will feel comfortable and look great in. Remember you will look back at your pictures from your big day for many years and you want everyone to look their best!

CHAPTER 19

DRESSING THE BRIDESMAIDS

LISA BRUMM

So you've chosen your wedding gown! Now it's time to get the perfect gown for your bridesmaids. You'll see many choices not only in style but colors and fabrics as well. Before taking your maid of honor or bridesmaids shopping, doing some homework will save you time and help keep your sanity. Many brides have shared with us over the years how frustrating and disappointing the bridesmaid shopping experience can be for everyone involved. Everyone is so excited to participate, but not everyone has the same taste, is the same size or has the same budget. So working on finding the "look" you want before shopping will go a long way in helping you enjoy the process.

The best place to start your bridesmaid gown search is in bridal magazines, wedding planning books and pictures of actual weddings online. Just like your wedding gown search, you'll want to have a clear vision of what your whole wedding will look and feel like. Will it be an early afternoon wedding, held under a beautiful tent on a hill overlooking a winery or golf course? Maybe you'll have an elegant affair, in your family church with a reception in a gorgeous banquet facility. Even a wedding held on your favorite beach! No matter where your wedding is to be held, you'll want a clear vision of the entire look and feel, so that when you are shopping with your maids, you can zero in on the perfect gown style for all of your bridesmaids. You've made a big start by booking your wedding ceremony facility as well as your reception venue. Then you purchased your bridal gown. These major decisions were based on your overall theme and feel of your personal vision for your amazing wedding day. Now let's get down to business, shopping for the maids!

You might want to bring only your maid of honor with you on the first visit. This can be a special time for just the two of you to connect and work together for your goal of finding that perfect bridesmaid gown. Make sure you make an appointment at your local bridal salon. You'll get better service and you will have a dedicated dressing room and consultant waiting for you when you arrive. You should also consider purchasing your bridesmaid dresses from the store where you purchased your bridal gown; many full service salons will offer special discounts and extra incentives to your maids because you have purchased your gown from them. Another benefit from purchasing at the same salon is trying on your gown with the maid's gowns so you can envision your entire look. Your bridal consultant is also in tune with your desires and you won't have to keep explaining your wants and needs over and over again.

There are four major gown silhouettes to consider for your maids, just as there were for your wedding gown. Every bride has many maids in her wedding with all different sizes and body shapes. Not to worry, since there are only four silhouettes to look at, it won't be as hard as you think. We know that a bridesmaid has concerns about the cost of the gown as well as alteration fees, hair and nail appointments and other costs associated with the wedding. So we'll make sure we take a look at how you can help your maids save money as well as time. By the end of this chapter you'll be prepared to jump into the bridesmaid shopping experience with an arsenal of information to help you find the perfect gown for your favorite bridesmaids!

So let's take a look at those four silhouettes and discuss the benefits of each style. Then we will tackle the whole issue of skirt lengths, colors, fabric choices, prices and more. Our first suggestion is to make sure when you and your maid of honor go shopping that you are aware of the four major silhouettes and that you try them all on to see what is available and what silhouette will be best for your bridesmaids. Sometimes a combination of silhouettes can be chosen with the same fabric and color, yet allowing each maid to look her best in the silhouette and neckline for her.

The first one up is the A-line or princess silhouette. The most versatile and flattering of all the formal dress styles, it is fitted around the bodice and upper waits and then it flares out into an "A" shape as it cascades to the floor dropping from the natural waistline.

This A-Line style is wildly popular as it is flattering to just about any figure, no matter what your body type. This style is fantastic for the pear shaped bridesmaids because it fits close to the natural curves of the bodice, accentuating their bust line, while camouflaging their lower half. The skirt styles of the A-line will range from a slimmer fit to a full cut A-line skirt. The best part of this style is how it flares out directly below the natural waistline, which can hide a heavier bum or hipline. The A-line will also flatter most of your fuller figured or full-busted bridesmaids. And when found in a heavier fabric, such as a satin, this style is especially flattering, because it won't cling. One of the best features of this style is how it creates an illusion of height on a shorter body, by elongating the bridesmaid's torso because it has no waistline seam. It's great at hugging the natural curves of the upper body. You'll find that the neckline associated with the A-line/princess style can range from the strapless, tank and halter style. All necklines look amazing with the A-line body silhouette. No wonder this ranks as one of the top picked silhouettes for bridesmaids. This silhouette allows for plenty of choices for each of your maids to choose from. If you wish for each maid to find a gown, yet choose a neckline that suits them best, then this is the silhouette for your bridesmaids.

Our second silhouette is the empire waist silhouette which is created by the waistline created just below the bust line. The word empire refers to the period of the First French Empire. However early examples of the style can be seen from early Greco-Roman period, where women wore gowns gathered just below their bust and fell gracefully to the floor. Many times this style is fashioned from a lighter fabric and flows beautifully allowing comfort and grace. For your bridesmaids with a thicker waistline, this style is very flattering and easily sweeps softly over curves. Your bridesmaid gown choices in the empire waist will be shown not only with strapless necklines, but with a tank strap neckline as well. Like the A-line, the empire waist can be very versatile for your bridesmaids and can accommodate whatever level of formality you choose for your wedding. The empire waist has made a great comeback and is not only popular for many figures, but can be seen in our ready to wear culture as well. Your empire waist style does fit very well on most body types, it is especially beautiful on those maids with smaller bust lines as well as good coverage for your fully busted bridesmaids. This is another great choice for each of your bridesmaids to wear.

Our third silhouette choice is the sheath style. This fitted style can flair below the hips and knees to give a "mermaid" or fit and flare look as well as falling in a graceful column to the floor. This sheath silhouette is very popular in the knee length as well, making it a great option for many wedding parties. Your sheath skirt does skim elegantly over curves and allows any size bridesmaid to look sleek and elegant. Your "mermaid" skirt is actually a great look for your ladies whether they have curves or no curves. The dropped waist with the flared lower skirt gives a curvier maid a sexy balanced look, while the maid with smaller or no curves, this mermaid silhouette gives her all the right curves in all the right places. A misconception that only slim figures can wear this silhouette is completely false. Any size figure looks amazing in a sheath or fitted skirt. The dropped waistline of a sheath is figure flattering and gives each bridesmaid a trim look that can actually allow the wearer to look like they've shed pounds. Any neckline looks fantastic with the sheath gown, so no worries on that front. Another fun fact about the knee length sheath skirts is pockets! Yes, pockets. You'll find that your maids will love having those little hidden pockets. What a fun option for your bridesmaid gowns.

Our final silhouette is the traditional Ball Gown silhouette. This might be one of the most dramatic and formal looks you can find for your bridesmaids. However, many knee length ball gowns work very well for an informal wedding, or a wedding taking place in a garden on a lovely summer afternoon. This classic and elegant look is composed of a form-fitting bodice that leads to a natural or slightly dropped waistline. The skirt is usually full, but not necessarily too full, especially on a bridesmaid gown. Many ball gowns for the bridesmaid have pretty sashes or belts that can lend a contrasting color or tone, allowing you to highlight another color from your wedding color selections. Much like the A-line silhouette, it flatters most figures and is especially good at hiding fuller hips, but not to worry about maids with smaller hips, the ball gown is also great at giving everyone a small waist and great curves. Your ball gown silhouette looks great in all fabrics, but most especially when made in chiffon, organza and taffeta. If you are not fond of the crinoline built into many of the skirts, it can always be easily removed by your seamstress for a less full look.

Now that we've discussed all the great gown silhouettes, let's move on to the skirt lengths and fabrics. Skirt lengths are really your choice, however when looking at bridal etiquette, you'll find there are some opinions on all the lengths, so let's discuss some of them, especially if you are feeling ambivalent about the length you want your maids to wear.

Traditionally when your wedding or reception is held after 4pm, then skirt lengths are usually to the floor. Hence the saying, "wedding after four, skirt lengths to the floor". Often weddings held in late afternoon or evening are more formal compared to weddings held earlier in the day. So knowing the time of your wedding helps you to choose your skirt lengths for the maids. There are three skirt lengths you may choose from, floor length, tea length and knee length. Your floor length gowns look very elegant and slightly more formal, and allow your bridesmaids to wear shoes that don't necessarily have to match, since very little of their shoes will actually show. Tea length gowns while not as popular are dressy as well as easy to wear. The actual length of tea length gowns ranges from just a couple inches above the ankle, to just a few inches below the knee. Many weddings held in the afternoon or in an informal setting take advantage of the tea length gowns and look fabulous.

The shorter knee length style gown has grown very popular in recent years and is seen at formal weddings as well as informal weddings. Commonly called the "cocktail" dress, this length gown can be worn again and again, so they become a great option for your maids. The knee length gown typically falls around the knee, sometimes just above the knee to just at the knee, depending on the actual style. These gowns normally don't need a hem, thus saving your bridesmaids money when it comes to alteration fees. When trying to be budget conscience for your bridesmaids this skirt length is fantastic, with wear ability after the wedding and eliminating the need for a hem, this would be a super choice.

With so many choices of color and fabric, it can seem overwhelming. But since you are doing your homework before your first visit, then this will be stress free! When working with brides I often find out if color is more important than the style, if so, you'll want to look at the color swatches available at the store you want to get your gowns from, before actually looking at gowns. Many times a bride will fall in love with a certain style, only to find out it does not come in the color she wants.

Let's talk about color...or rather all the names of the colors available. Such as the color "apple" can be red from one company and green from another. So don't get to hung up on the name of the color, but look at the actual fabric swatches to find the color you wish your maids to wear. Other color options found in bridesmaid gowns is two tone, or two colors in the gown. Such as a sash or belt in a contrasting color or a peek a boo hemline in a contrasting color. Small brooches or fabric flowers attached at the waistline are very attractive and add an appealing element to the bridesmaid gowns. Your bridal consultant is a great asset when it comes to knowing what options are available to you with each gown company and can make great suggestions to help you choose the best look so make sure you ask a lot of questions.

The fabric of your bridesmaid gown is typically set in stone, meaning you can't change the fabric without a significant cost. But if you are drawn to a certain fabric, then make sure you let your consultant know so she can help you find the gowns in your color choice as well as your favorite fabric choices. Satin has always been a traditional choice for many brides over the years, but today, it's not your Mother's satin! Today's satin fabric is lighter weight, comes in more colors and looks fantastic in so many styles. Another great option is chiffon, which flows beautifully and is also available in many, many colors. Taffeta, which is available with darker iridescent tones as well as lighter tones, is a great formal fabric. When taffeta is used on a gown with ruching, it helps the wearer look amazing and helps to slim and trim the waistline. Jersey is a knit fabric, which has some cling to it, but can also flow nicely over the bust and hip. Organza is a sheer product with a little more stiffness to it, but looks great in the ball gown silhouette. Typically jersey and organza are not offered in as many colors as your satin, taffeta and chiffon.

Before we talk about pricing, just a few words about working with a bridal salon versus buying gowns online. The Internet is a great place to shop, research, chat, and keep tabs with all your friends and family. But just a word of caution on shopping for your bridal and bridesmaids gowns before we move on. Because this is one of the most important days you'll ever dress for, and because it can be so complicated due to styles, fabrics, colors and options, it's best to work with a reliable bridal salon. The staffs at your local bridal salon are trained and knowledgeable with all the complicated gown issues that arise and are more than willing to help you with your bridesmaid gowns as well as your bridal gown. These ladies at your local salon have helped to dress hundreds and hundreds of brides and their maids. They want to help you with your special needs, whether it's bridesmaids who live out of state, a maid with a disability, maids in all sizes, and any other special requests. The stores on the Internet don't have gowns for you to try on; they can't show you actual fabric swatches. They are interested in selling you a gown for as low a price as they can, while not understanding all your needs. And because bridesmaid gowns must be made, these gowns are not returnable and non-refundable. So if your maid orders the wrong size because she was not measured properly, she'll be in quite a bind. The savings you thought you were making, actually turn out to be more of a headache and more costly than anticipated.

Pricing on bridesmaids gowns run from approximately $130.00 to over $300.00 and everything in between. When you and your maid of honor make your first visit to your local bridal salon, remember to discuss openly what your budget would be for your maids. Allow the consultant to show you options in your budget and if nothing appeals to you in that price range, don't be afraid to let your consultant know you'd like to look at gowns just slightly higher in price. Your consultant wants you and your maids to be happy with the gown style, color, fabric and price. Alterations are another consideration for each bridesmaid, and actually a well-made bridesmaid gown may require fewer alterations because of a better fit. Typically this gown would cost more up front because of better gown construction, but savings on the alterations balance out, and most customers are happier with the look and fit of this type of gown. Typically the cheaper the gown is, the less gown construction there is and this can affect the look of the gown. Most stores will require payment in full before ordering the bridesmaid gowns. And if all the maids are in the same color or colors, the order for the gowns will not be placed until all your maids have been measured and down payments are made. The time frame for the gowns to be made and shipped to the store may vary, but the average is 12-16 weeks. And don't forget your maids will need to have their gowns altered, which depending on the season can take anywhere from 4-8 weeks to accomplish. So please remember that you'll need to order your bridesmaid gowns at least 6-8 months before your wedding. But not to worry if you find yourself 5-6 months out from your wedding and you haven't placed your bridesmaid order. You can pay to have the gowns put on a rush status. It will cost each bridesmaid approximately $25.00-$50.00 each, but the ship dates on a rush can be just 5-7 weeks, saving you some time. It does pay to plan ahead, but rush cuts are available with many bridesmaid companies. So don't panic! Your consultant will advise you on your choices and understands the ship date process.

So to wrap all this up and give you some last words of encouragement before you go bridesmaid shopping, I'll give you some condensed pointers. Please take this book with you on all your shopping events, and don't be afraid to refer back to each chapter as you progress in your wedding planning.

- Make sure you do your homework and look at pictures to draw inspiration for your own wedding.

- Think about the time, season and the place you will get married and how the bridesmaid gowns will fit in.

- Call or e-mail the bridal shop where you purchased your gown to set up an initial appointment to look at bridesmaid gowns with your maid of honor. Remember too many cooks can spoil the soup!

- Once you and your maid of honor have found a small selection of styles, make your final appointment to bring your maids in to finalize the choice of gown.

- When you've made the final choice make sure your bridesmaids bring money to make their down payment. Most bridal salons will not measure your maids without a down payment.

- Ask for a swatch of the color once you've placed your bridesmaid order so you can use that when planning your decorations and flowers.

- Find out the final cut off date to have all your maids get their gown ordered. Make sure all your maids understand the gowns must be ordered by that date; otherwise they might delay the gowns arrival.

- Ask your consultant how they can help your out of town or out of state bridesmaids get their gown ordered.

- Your consultant will be able to give you an approximate ship date once ALL your maids have been measured and their down payments have been made. Remember ship dates are approximate and gowns may arrive on, before or after the ship date you are given.

Ok! You are ready to go out there and find the perfect bridesmaid gown. Remember to enjoy the process and have fun. That's what planning a wedding should be, fun, enjoyable and stress free.

CHAPTER 20

DRESSING THE OTHER GUESTS (MOTHERS AND CHILDREN) AND FASHION TIPS FOR MOTHERS

ELODIA ADAMSON

Bridal store experts and stylists have the honor and yet difficult duty of dressing brides for the most important day of their lives. However, there are many other important people in the wedding party that need to be dressed as well. The bridesmaids play a key role in the wedding ceremony and party as do the flower girls and of course, the mother of the bride and the mother of the groom. Here is some guidance on how to dress some of these important members of the wedding party.

The Mother of the Bride (this advice is also useful for the mother of the groom)

Age Appropriate

One of the most important things to keep in mind when selecting a mother of the bride gown or suit is to be mindful of one's age. While it is understandable that a mother of the bride wants to impress her guests (many guests of the wedding party are the mother of the bride's lifelong friends and often their ex-husband), a mother of the bride should look age appropriate and should never upstage the bride. The role of the mother of the bride is to support her daughter on her wedding day and entertain her guests at the reception. While she should select a gown or dress that makes her look elegant, chic, and fashionable, her selection should follow the trend set by the bride's gown selection and choice in bridesmaid dresses.

Things to avoid are cleavage (all eyes need to be on the bride), a dress with a train, and a gown that is more elaborate than the bride's. When selecting a sleeveless, strapless, or halter gown, women should keep in mind the shape of their arms and consider some arm exercises with weights a few months prior to the big day (God forbid your sorority sisters gossip about your arms not being toned). A mother of the bride dress should never have a train as she is not the one walking down the aisle.

Follow the Wedding Theme

Traditionally, the mother of the bride sets the trend for what both mother of the bride and groom will wear, however the bride and groom decide if the wedding is formal/black-tie, cocktail, a daytime affair, or a garden wedding. All members of the bridal party should dress accordingly and follow the tone that has been set. If a bride selects a very simple and elegant gown with no sequins or embroidery, the mother of the bride should consider a dress that is not embellished in order to not outshine the bride. If the bride selects a straight gown, the mother of the bride should refrain from wearing a ball gown which would certainly upstage the bride. Formal weddings mean that all guests should wear a long dress. A cocktail wedding can have guests dressed in long or short gowns. However, if the mother of the bride selects a long gown, the mother of the groom is supposed to follow her lead and wear a long gown. Same goes if the mother of the bride selects a short gown. You may ask why this is the rule. The reason for this is that the photographer will photograph the bride and groom with both sets of parents and the photographs will appear unbalanced if one mom is showing her legs and the other is not. Pantsuits are acceptable; there are many pantsuits on the market today that are formal and appropriate for even the most formal affair.

Please note that the mother of the bride and mother of the groom need not have the same length of dress as the bridesmaids as they are rarely photographed together.

Attractive not Sexy
While the mother of the bride has every right to want to look her best, one absolute no-no is cleavage or any dress that is overly sexy. The same would be advised when selecting a bridesmaid dress. This is the bride's big day and all eyes should be on her. If selecting a short dress, sticking to the age appropriateness rule will ensure that the mother of the bride doesn't select a mini-cocktail dress. Sometimes it is not how revealing a dress is that makes it overly provocative; at times it is the fit of the gown which tends to stop traffic. A mother of the bride should pay attention to sizing and select a dress that fits her shape without being overly tight or snug. This is not the time to get revenge on your ex-husband and his new wife or to show-off your body to your ex-college roommates.

Are strapless and halter top gowns appropriate for the mother of the bride? There are different schools of thought. In general, strapless and halter top gowns evoke overt sexiness which is what we are trying to avoid. However, every woman with a spectacular figure has every right to show it off. If a mother of the bride is in superb shape, strapless and halter gowns are appropriate. For women who aren't the same size as they were in high school, they may consider a strapless dress that includes a bolero or shawl which will cover their arms. Also recommended are dresses with straps, sleeves, or off the shoulder. If one follows the age appropriateness rule, strapless gowns and halter top dresses are appropriate if the mother of the bride is genetically gifted with stellar arms, back, and shoulders, or is highly motivated and spends countless hours at the gym.

Comfort and Confidence

Most important in selecting a mother of the bride gown or mother of the groom is the mother's own level of comfort. It is important that she feels confident and is in a dress that suits her sense of style and personality. This is her daughter's day to be married but it is also a big day for the mother of the bride. She will presumably host many family and friends and as the hostess, she needs to look her best and glow in a gown that she is very comfortable in.

This is a good time to discuss size. Many women are not happy with their size and often refuse to move up in size swearing they are going to lose the weight. Accepting one's size and selecting a dress that fits is more important than the number on the tag inside the dress. No woman is comfortable in a dress that doesn't really fit her nor does she look great in it. A happy and comfortable mother of the bride will glow regardless of the size of her dress.

Another key element of comfort is the SHOES. The mother of the bride and mother of the groom must be mindful of the comfort of the shoes they select. There is nothing worse than a beautiful woman in a horrible mood because her feet hurt. If the mother of the bride's feet are in pain, people will look at her sad face and not her shoes. The mother of the bride or mother of the groom will be on their feet for countless hours on the big day and on the days before the wedding; tired feet are a given so be mindful when making the selection.

Colors

The wedding colors set the tone for the wedding ceremony as they are seen throughout the event in the flowers, bridesmaid gowns, table linens, party favors and more. The mother of the bride can wear a color complimentary to the bridesmaids; however, if the color selected for the bridesmaids is not a color that suits her well, it is advisable for her to select a different hue so long as it doesn't clash. Please try not to have the entire wedding party look like a Las Vegas hotel carpet pattern. So long as the alternative color does not clash the overall color scheme, it is a better choice to select a color that looks good on the mother of the bride's skin tone and one that she is comfortable in. In recent years black has become the choice color for bridesmaid dresses and dresses for the mother of the bride and mother of the groom. While black is Coco Chanel's greatest contribution to women's fashion, most photographers will say that it is not the best color for photos. Additionally, it is not the most joyous color for what is supposed to be the happiest day in a daughter's life. Therefore, it is strongly suggested that the mother of the bride at least consider wearing a color that suits her hair and skin tone. If your hair is silver DO NOT wear a silver dress; if you are a blonde, avoid a gold dress. Why? Much of the ceremony has the mother of the bride giving her back to the guests and one does not want their head blending into the entire gown losing the silhouette.

Color can greatly affect how slim a person looks. For heavy set and plus size women, pastels are normally not recommended, but if it makes you happy, it is not a problem. Also stay away from all prints; they really aren't as formal and elegant as a solid. Jewel tones are wonderful in fall and winter and elegant neutrals such as pewter, green, blue, and shades of brown and champagne are perfect all year round.

As for white or ivory, the only ones wearing white or ivory at a wedding are the bride and the flower girl. It's amazing and quite frankly, appalling to see people still continue to break this rule. There is an exception to this; brides are having winter white weddings or beach weddings and they ask all guests to wear white and ivory.

Fabric
When it comes to fabric selection, the easiest rules are "NO VELVET" unless it's winter and it's really cold outside and "NO TULLE" unless

you're a ballerina and under 25 years old. The rest is fair game. The mother of the bride will be moving around before and during the ceremony so it is advisable to select gowns that don't tend to wrinkle as much as others. Overly shiny materials are not helpful when trying to look slim and should be avoided. However, if the bridesmaid dresses are velvet and the mother of the bride is a plus size woman, DO NOT go with velvet which makes one look heavier due to its thickness and texture. Brocades are lovely but also tend to be thick and heavier than most fabrics – there is a very fine line between an elegant brocade and a fabric that would be best on a sofa.

Mother of the Groom

It is advisable for the mother of the groom to follow the same advice and suggestions provided for the mother of the bride. Her role is similar as she too is a hostess to her family and friends attending her son's wedding. The mother of the bride and the mother of the groom's gowns should complement one another and may be similar in color and or style. Their gowns may also contrast one another so long as they don't clash. Remember no need to match; simply don't clash. This helps stage better photo opportunities when the photographer poses the entire wedding party.

Flower Girls

Flower girls are a delightful addition to a wedding party. Their role comes at the beginning of the ceremony and always draws attention as they sweetly walk down the aisle preceding the bride. Their dresses should be sweet and youthful and compliment the bride's gown; they can often mimic the bridal gown in terms of the material, color, and details.

The most important thing to consider for the flower girls is their comfort. While they play an important role, one should remember that the flower girls are playful children and need to be as comfortable as possible so that they can get through the ceremony in a joyful mood. Please avoid any type of itchy fabric as this is very annoying to anyone, especially a child. Also make sure that the child can easily go potty without the disturbance of petty coats and layers and layers of tulle. The worst that can happen is for a flower girl to throw a tantrum five minutes before the bride is about to walk down the aisle.

In recent years, children's fashion has delivered to the market some very provocative attire bordering on hoochie-mama status. Perhaps its old fashioned to think that Brittney Spears and Jessica Simpson have no business designing one inch heels for little girls but it's simply a reality. Toddlers and Tiaras are not the look one should aspire to when dressing a flower girl. This is not a time for them to be dressing up in princess costume and halter dresses and strapless gowns aren't appropriate for children and neither is make-up.

Guests
Most wedding invitations today will indicate if a wedding is black-tie/formal, black-tie optional, or cocktail. When a wedding is designated as formal or black-tie, men should dress in a tuxedo and women should wear floor length gowns. Black-tie optional gives guests the option of wearing a long gown or a short cocktail dress. Cocktail indicates that it is a dressy affair only not one for formal attire.

Many weddings today are in destinations such as beach resorts or vineyards. This in no way means the wedding is not formal. If the invitation indicates the affair is formal, guests should follow that request while finding attire that is appropriate for the affair and also fits the weather and setting for the event. Destination weddings often have outside ceremonies and some are even on the beach. Try to find a dress that doesn't look awkward worn outside; an example of a mismatch would be a velvet gown or something overly beaded on a beach.

Enjoy the Wedding
The best advice a wedding expert can give any wedding guest is to enjoy the wedding. Select a gown that looks good on YOU! Find a color and style that accentuates the best features and has you exude confidence. Stick with your "look" and personality by selecting a dress that you feel

good in. Look for a dress that you would wearas a guest of the wedding, only dressier. Have a great time and smile for the pictures.

In a Nutshell

- Dress age-appropriate

- No cleavage or mini-skirt length dresses

- For formal and cocktail affairs, pantsuits are acceptable.

- Colors need not match; they just must not clash

- Wear your size; avoid looking like a stuffed sausage

- Comfort is key; it's going to be a long day

- Jewel tones are the best choice for plus sized women

- Velvet is only for winter

- White is always a NO NO (exception to the rule)

- Long dresses make women look taller and slimmer

- Get those arms in shape if you want to wear strapless or halter

- No make-up or itchy fabric on flower girls; they're children!

- Enjoy the Day!!!

CHAPTER 21

THE CEREMONY: GETTING READY (COUNTDOWN AND CHECK LIST) - TIPS ON PHOTOGRAPHY FOR YOUR GOWN

DOMINIQUE LEVESQUE

You have been planning this day for months even perhaps years. By now you should be excited and elated that everything is coming together. Your family and friends are showering you with gifts, love and support. The atmosphere is palpable. You have high expectations and you will need all the help you can get to pull this day together. Your friends and family can be a great resource of help for that special day. Many of the brides I see in the boutique try to do everything on their own and that can be a recipe for disaster. They take on too many DIY's, leave too many things to the last minute, and don't know when to ask for help. In this chapter I will cover many little things that you need to think about on that day from delegating, photography tips, scheduling and much more. Hopefully these tips will help bring your vision to life, keep your spirits up, help you avoid costly mistakes and create memories that will last for a lifetime.

Preparing your gown:

Many of our customers get confused at this step and feel a little lost. These days the majority of us are not used to going to a seamstress to have our garments altered. We have so many choices available to us in stores that if it doesn't fit most of us will not buy it. So in many cases our brides are overwhelmed at this very important step. At the bridal salon when we receive your gown we will press it for your viewing and pick-up. After trying on your gown, you may decide that some alterations are needed to achieve a perfect fit. In our store we recommend that alterations should be performed six to twelve weeks prior to the wedding depending on the time of year. This will ensure you have time to look over all the details, and it will help you cut down on the running around the week of the wedding. In most cases you may need two to three appointments to complete the work. After alterations are done the seamstress will press your gown to remove the wrinkles that may have occurred during the sewing process. When the dress is ready to take home, it would be ideal (if the wedding is less then a week away) to hang your dress out of the bag with the train laid out properly. It will help to keep it wrinkle free. Make sure the place where you decide to hang your dress is safe, from pets for example.

If you are traveling with your gown you may have to plan alternatives to ensure that your dress is in pristine condition to walk down the aisle. If you are traveling to a resort that specializes in wedding packages, they normally have the proper steaming equipment to ensure professional results. In this case it would be important to communicate ahead of time with your resort to let them know that you may require this service. Usually it's not a problem, but keep in mind that they have a high volume of weddings every week so communicating with them will ensure special attention will be given to your gown.

If that service is not available for you from the hotel, or perhaps you are staying with a relative, here are some options for you:

- Local bridal shops often offer steaming services to out of town brides. To ensure they will have sufficient time to steam your gown, be sure to call ahead. Keep in mind that steaming a gown may take a few hours and it needs time to dry for best results.

- Steaming the gown yourself is also an option. You can purchase domestic steamers in department stores. They come in different sizes, from handheld travel size to upright steamers with valet attachments. I recommend you start using your steamer on several occasions prior to using it on your wedding gown. Not every one is comfortable with steamers. You may ask the bridal salon where you purchased your gown if they could show you some hints to achieve professional results. Like in every thing else, practice makes perfect and patience is essential. Even if you decide to have it steamed professionally, having your own steamer on the wedding day would make last minute touch ups possible.

Many brides ask me if they can use their iron on the wedding gown. I answer this one with words of caution. On most fabrics the iron may be used with out problems, as long as you know how to set your iron to the proper temperature. If you had your gown altered, ask to keep the fabric remnants. You will be able to use them to test your iron. I strongly suggest that you never ever use the hotel iron directly on your gown. Most of the time, these irons are not properly maintained. For example they may have dirty water or even worse rust in them, and you really do not want that on your gown. Wrinkles are better then a rusty iron mark in my opinion.

"How To"
Here is the "how to" properly lace up and fasten your gown section. You will not be lacing or buttoning your own, but perhaps you will have to help your bridesmaids or mom with their gown or teach them how to do yours.

For the lace up:

- First, step in with the gown completely unlaced.

- Second, insert the laces in top loops from the outside in and even out the length on each side.

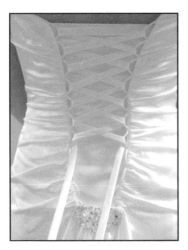

- Keep on inserting the laces in the loops form the outside in; making sure to not twist the lace to give it a flawless look.

- Pull on lace to tighten until you reach the desired fit. You may have to repeat this step more then once to reach comfort.

- Depending on your gown you can choose to make a knot at the bottom and tuck the laces in the gown or you may do a bow and some gown are designed to cover the end of the lace up.
- Your gown may have an inside corset. If so you can use the same technique as mentioned above.

If you have buttons and loops:

· If your gown has a functional button detail at the back with loops to fasten, a great tool to have on hand is a crochet hook. A crochet hook will facilitate the task as well as save your manicure.

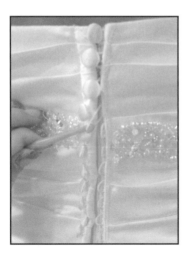

Money

Many of the vendors require payment before or cash on the day of. If you ignore this detail you may very well set yourself up for heated arguments on your wedding day. For you it's a very special day, you want to make sure to keep all of your vendors happy so they can help you make your vision come true. Keep in mind that for them it's how they make their living, this represents their pay check for services rendered so you can't ask them to be lenient with you.

The reason many vendors want to be paid in full before the wedding or will only accept cash the day of (no checks or credit cards) is they have just had too many missed payments. To ensure a good atmosphere, go through your list of vendors with balances left to pay and doublecheck who needs payment the day of and which one will give you extensions if needed and which one should you pay ahead. Keeping track of your expenses is key on that day. Bouncing checks reflects poorly on your banking, credit score and may prevent you from getting credit in the future (such as a mortgage).

If this step is mismanaged you could have undesirable repercussions that would affect you beyond your wedding day.

Creating Moments:
Your wedding day is so important and filled with expectations, not just from the couple getting married but from everyone who loves them, mom and dad, brothers, sisters and close friends. If you can manage to include some special times to spend with them in your schedule you will create memories that will last you a life time. You can prepare sentimental cards or small token gifts to give out that day to just let them know how important they are to you. These moments will be cherished for a lifetime.

The Groom
Have you included your spouse in all of the wedding planning? Whether you have or not it is important that every one is on the same page that day. Both of you should have the schedule of the other. The bride often feels that she has too much to do that day, but the groom has time to go play a leisurely game of golf in the morning. Each of you will have their own way of making this day special for one another and

your loved ones which is why communication is so important. If you take the time to figure out the details and split the "to do" list you will feel that each other is equally involved and dedicated in making this day memorable. After all, neither of you are mind readers, communication will give you a clear understanding of the other's expectations.

Bouquet and Garter Toss

Funny traditions surround the tossing of the bride's bouquet and garter to unmarried friends. The tosses usually happen before the cake cutting or toward the end of the celebration, just before the couple leaves. Photographers at the wedding love to take these photos since everyone is having a good time by then.

The superstition of the bouquet toss is that whoever catches the bride's bouquet is the next one to be married. The bride usually goes to the center of the dance floor or up a few stairs. She either faces the group of single female guests or turns her back and tosses the bouquet over her head into the group.

If you're planning to save your bouquet, ask your florist to create a breakaway or a separate smaller bouquet for you to toss.

If you have live musicians, they usually play "tossing" music (drum rolls), and a sting (cymbals) when the bouquet is caught. The winning lady then waits to see which man is going to catch the toss of the garter, as that is whom she is going to dance with next.

For the garter toss the bride sits on a chair, usually in the middle of the dance floor. The groom lifts her skirt up to remove her garter which she is wearing just above her knee on the right leg, slipping it off her leg with his hands. Depending on the groom's antics, this tradition is fun and usually creates laughter. If there is a live band, the musicians know exactly what to play. The groom then swirls it around until he lets it go into the group of unmarried male guests. The garter catcher then dances with the bouquet catcher.

If for some reason you don't want to have either of these tosses at your wedding, just eliminate them. Some brides present their maid of honour with a separate bouquet in private to toss as an option.

Photography Tips

When you picked your wedding gown did you think of how it would look in your photos? Most likely that was one of your priorities, the drape of the fabric, just the right amount of sparkle and how the cut of the gown made your best features standout. It is just as important when you pick colors for your bridesmaids and mothers. I often see brides imposing colors while not thinking of the impact on the portraits. I had a bride once that told me she absolutely wanted dark navy for her bridesmaids because they needed to mach the carpet and drapes from the venue. Please think about that for a second. I understand that you want things to coordinate well, but keeping a very monochrome palate will hide all the details you spent so much time creating. Nothing will stand out, and there will be no point of interest in your photos.

When it comes to color choices, think of where you want your photos to be taken. Go and visit these places, don't just rely on the photographer's portfolio. It can give you ideas, but do your own legwork. See the colors that surround you. What stands out for you? If you have some idea of what you want for your color scheme bring color swatches (like the one from the paint store) with you. It will give you a great indicator of what will work for you and your bridal party.

Not all moms look good in pastel or taupe. When an event such as a wedding comes along moms often want to play it safe. What I hear most often from my customers is that they want something simple to avoid upstaging the bride. They choose soft colors to try to blend into the background. This is not the time ladies! These portraits are your memories; they will be around for a long time. Look for colors that will suit the skin tones and don't be afraid to try something new. You might surprise yourself.

You and your photographer may have discussed what photos you want for the day, just remember to write down a list of all of the people you want to have photos with. Too many times, brides don't do this and see their wedding day pictures without certain friends and family that they really wanted to take a picture with. Write this list down for your photographer and try to take the pictures right after the ceremony so you will at least have one picture to remember the day with your guests.

Did you choose a veil to go with your wedding dress? If you didn't you might want to reconsider. There are so many different styles these days, the finger tip, bird cage, cathedral, one, two, or three tiers: you can surely find one that suits your style. The veil is an excellent accessory for your wedding photos. The big advantage to having a veil is that it frames the face really nicely, especially on the close ups.

Great shoes and funky accessories are a fun way for your photographer to capture your personality. They do not need to be the ones you will wear down the aisle necessarily. One of my brides took pictures with her mom's original headpiece. It was for sentimental reasons and the photographer took the photos as they were getting ready in the morning. It added great interest to her photo album.

Pre-Wedding Portraits:
On the big day the timeline is tight. Many of our brides who are wanting either many locations for their photos or the ideal location is not close to the chosen venue, are opting for pre-wedding portraits. If you choose to go that route here are some things to keep in mind.

The pros:
- More relaxed environment since you are not on such a tight deadline
- You can experiment with the photographer more freely
- You can choose as many locations as budget and time can allow
- You get to see if there is any thing you would like to change for the day of (e.g.: the hair did not hold up, the color of the flowers did not look as great as you thought, etc.)

- On your wedding day you will enjoy having more time with your guests
- If the weather does not cooperate on your wedding day, you know you already have great photos
- You get to enjoy your dress one extra day!!!

The cons:
- Pre-wedding photo shoots require a lot of planning
- Your wedding party might not all be available
- Your wedding gown and your bridesmaids' dresses will probably need to be cleaned or repressed before your wedding day.
- What if you damage your gown?
- Extra tux rental
- For the superstitious in your family this represents bad luck
- The cost!

If you do choose the pre-wedding portraits make sure you set up gown pressing appointments with your bridal salon ahead of time. There are extra costs for those services but it is so important that professionals handle your gown. They will be able to see if any thing needs repair so you can attend to it before the wedding day. You want to walk down the aisle in pristine condition no one needs to know it's the second time you've worn it.

Schedule!!!

This is one of the most important things a bride should do. Create a schedule, but beyond that, distribute it to your bridal party, family and friends. One of my friends even had a family meeting to walk through the wedding day schedule with them. All of this helped her family to be more prepared on the big day and helped them remain calm. She didn't get any questions like "What's next?", "What's going on?", "Where should I stand?" Creating a schedule will bring clarity, peace of mind and may save your friendships along the way. You must make it as detailed as possible and make sure you include time for yourself to enjoy every moment of this very special day. Give a copy to everyone, review it, and post it everywhere.

To make it easier, you must delegate either by asking who would like to take on certain things or by assigning specific tasks. Keep in mind that your wedding party will be busy too, with photos, hair, make up, etc., so limit to no more then two tasks each. They will have enough on their minds. Too many tasks will result in things being forgotten, skipped over, or just running out of time. It's the perfect opportunity to reach out to your close friends, cousins, aunts... to assume the rest of the details.

Here is a list of things you should include in your day-of schedule:

Breakfast:
- Keeping yourself well nourished will help with your energy levels
- Don't drink too much coffee (it will dehydrate you)
- If you choose to drink a mimosa or a glass of champagne, please do so in moderation

Shower:
- Sounds simple but you have to make time for it

Hairstylist and Makeup:
- Have a sample color and photo of your gown to help your stylist and makeup artist.
- Wear a button down shirt so you can easily take it off without ruining the hair and makeup.
- If you're using an in home service make sure you have a proper space for them to set up. You should consider that they will need light, mirrors, and a table to set up as well as proper electricity.
- If you are using a local beauty salon make sure to calculate travel time.
- Call before leaving the house to make sure the salon is not running late.
- Have your head piece and veil on hand and ready to go.

Arrival of Bridesmaids:
- Some brides prefer starting the day with her bridesmaids at the hair and makeup appointment and some prefer to have them come a little later. Make sure you have everyone's cell phone numbers on hand in case of a last minute emergency.
- This is a great time to exchange gifts with your bridal party.

Arrival of Photographer and Videographer:
- They will need some time to setup the lights and choose the angles where they will photograph.
- If you have specific areas you want photographed (e.g., mom and dad in front of the fireplace) you should have a list and make sure to let your photographer know right away. This would be a great task to delegate.

Getting Dressed:
- Go to the washroom before you get dressed. You might find it difficult to use the facilities after the gown is on, plus you want to keep the gown clean. At my friends wedding many girls were using the washroom as their makeup room. That floor was in no condition to be touched by a wedding dress.
- If you need to wear a crinoline, petticoat, or slip make sure it goes on before the dress.
- If you have a lace-up gown, make sure someone with you that day knows how you want it done.
- Don't put the dress on too tight, you need to be able to breathe and sit down.
- Before leaving the house you should verify how to bustle your gown and show a trusted person how to help you with it when it's time.

Transportation Arrival Time (limousine, horse and carriage...):
- Before leaving the house, make sure you have every thing you need with you. A checklist can help you with that. This is a great task to delegate.

- Enter and exit the vehicle with care and precaution. You have spent all morning trying to keep your gown clean and wrinkle free, the car ride can make all your efforts go to waste. Your wedding party can be of great help at this step.

Ceremony:
- Before your big entrance doublecheck that your crinoline has not shifted. This is the number one reason brides' trip and stumble down the aisle.
- Shake off the train to give it fullness. It will also release some of the small creasing that could have occurred during the car ride.
- Delicately place the veil in the desired look.
- Touch up lipstick if need be.
- Don't forget to breathe.

Snacks:
- After the ceremony you and your wedding party will have released a lot of stress, you will need a boost of energy. Light snacks will keep the mood up for the photo session and tie you over until the reception. It doesn't have to be catered and fancy. It could be little snack bags for each member. Your wedding party will find it very thoughtful and they will enjoy the photo session much more.
- Don't forget to hydrate throughout the day; it will keep your skin radiant.

The Reception:
- When is it time to bustle my gown? Most of my brides bustle the gown before they make their big entrance in the hall as Ms. and Mrs. With that being said, you could bustle it up to suit the flow of your reception. It could be after the first dance or when you cut the cake... don't forget to let the chosen person know when you will need her help.
- Did you plan for a second dress? This is a trend that has been making a big comeback. The second gown is often a much simpler

gown or a very fun short little number. Many of my brides take this opportunity to have fun with accessories such as colourful fasteners for their hair and long strands of accent color beads to show their personality.

- Shoes are an important part of your day. Make sure to choose a shoe that will be comfortable for the whole day, there is nothing worse then having sore feet. If you decided to go for fashion versus comfort consider a shoe to change into for dancing like a ballet flat or flip flops.

Over Night Bag:

- Plan your overnight bag in advance so you are not scrambling last minute and forget important things such as makeup remover (that would make for a scary morning).

Coordinator Wanted:

If you find that planning and organizing is really not your strong suit, the concept of the whole day frightens you, and that requesting help from friends and family is not what you had in mind, perhaps a day-of coordinators services are right for you.

A full on wedding planner for your wedding was perhaps financially out of reach, but did you know you could hire help for the day of only? Day-of coordinators are a great alternative that is available at a fraction of the cost and will bring you peace of mind.

"Day-of packages and other partial services are becoming the norm as wedding consultants try to draw in couples of all budget points. And it's working. This year, 21 percent of those marrying will use a wedding planner, with nearly half of them requesting the day-of service, according to Shane McMurray, author of the Wedding Report, a market research website."

There are so many components to keep in mind on your wedding day - from the ceremony, to the cocktail hour, to all the activities that take place during the reception. A professional coordinator makes sure you keep on schedule, maintains a great flow, handles any crises that may arise, and makes certain the day is worry and stress free for you. If this is a service you can afford I highly recommend it. It will take an immense load off your shoulders, leave you more time to enjoy your family and friends, and make you look like a wedding maven.

This wonderful day will be filled with memories of joy and happiness if you are able to live in the moment. Try to take in all of the beauty of this day in a vision that will last you a lifetime. I hope the tips I have given you will help you to deal with the details and give you room to manage the stresses that may arise. Being well prepared will give you peace of mind and a sense of accomplishment that will contribute to your happy memories.

CHAPTER 22

UH OH: PREPARING FOR POSSIBLE EMERGENCIES AND WEDDING DISASTERS

ANDRAEA REED

So, you have spent the last few months preparing for one of the biggest days of your life, and in some cases the last couple of years. You have gone through every little detail from the color of the dessert napkins to which tux will look best next to you and your bridesmaids. Your venue was carefully chosen, and you fought over who sits at which table at the reception (because let's face it, your crazy uncle shouldn't be sitting at table number five with your nice friend from college). Every element of your wedding day has been accounted for. But what most brides do not spend months planning are the "what-if" scenarios.

One of the most important days of your life is full of those carefully planned details, and the last thing that any bride wants is for months of plans to unravel. Now, before we dive in with how to deal with possible emergencies, take into account that any number of things can go wrong. However, focus on the big ones. This is a "choose your battle" event. If you are missing one-hundred yellow dessert napkins, that's okay because your mother-in-law or the best man just showed up quite inebriated. Your guests will figure out how to clean up their dessert mess, so push the napkins to the back of your mind and delegate someone to grab some coffee and a chair in a separate room for your soon to be mother-in-law or your husband's ex best friend.

Delegating is the key to overcoming wedding day disasters. You don't have to fix all the situations that take place at the wedding you just have to have people around you that are willing to step up and make things right. In the case of the partying guest or relative, don't go near them as you risk too much with a white dress and perfect hair. Find someone to monitor them and get back to the moment you were caught up in.

This is just one scenario in which you can easily control the outcome. Now, let's talk about those small emergencies that no one really anticipates, but can be fixed if prepared for.

Your wedding gown should be one of the first things that you picked out. It is said, "Groom, wedding date, dress, venue, and everything after are just details." Your gown is one of the most important parts of your day. Every detail matters because you have spent so long working on them, but let's be honest: people are there to see you get married to the love of your life and most people will not remember details of the wedding. Some grooms don't even recall what color the bridesmaid dresses were! He will, however, remember you walking down that aisle toward him in the perfect wedding gown.

These are a few emergencies that can be anticipated and prepared for. A spot on the dress is a common emergency. Whether you get a spot before the ceremony or during the reception, it can be dealt with. Make sure that you have on hand: baby wipes, club soda, cheese cloth, a hair dryer, hair spray, a Tide Stain Stick, and white chalk if you have a silk dress.

Say that you get a makeup stain on your dress. Take the baby wipe and gently blot only the area of the stain to get it out. Do not use soap and water because this will make the stain more noticeable. Use the hair dryer once it is out to dry it quickly. If mascara is the culprit, use the cheesecloth and a little water, same procedure. If you get ink on your dress, you can actually use hairspray to lightly blot it out really easily. Red wine can be blotted gently with the club soda. Don't rub, just blot until it comes out. Now, if your dress is silk, do not try to rub, wipe, or wash anything out. You simply need to take white chalk and lightly cover the stain. Silk is such a delicate fabric, that getting it wet or trying to clean it can damage it permanently.

If your dress has a snag in it, the best thing you can do is simply let it go. Pulling on it will only make it worse, and chances of anyone seeing it are slim. If someone does happen to see the snag and says something to you, don't pounce. Just smile and thank them for coming then move on to other guests.

A common problem that brides face comes with the popular strapless gown. How often do you see girls tugging at their strapless dress trying to keep it from falling down? I have had many brides and mothers bring this concern up while wedding dress shopping. Here is what I tell them: "First of all, most of it is mental. Your dress will not fall down. The security of straps or sleeves that you are used to is gone, so it is only natural that you will want to make sure that nothing is going to fall. However, you should also feel secure in your dress. Make sure that you get a dress with built-in boning and bra. A lot of cheaper gowns do not have this and require that you buy the long-line bra instead. With a built in bra, the dress sits perfectly where it should on your waist and will not move." You also need to make sure that you get the right size. If your dress is too small, then the cups of the dress will pucker out so that they aren't flush against your skin. If the dress is too large, then it will feel like it is going to slip. Something to bring with you just in case is double-sided tape, or fashion tape. If you place this on the inside of the dress under the arms then the dress will stay in place a lot better.

Ultimately, the best thing you can do for that assured security is to buy a gown that is made with the built in bra.

The last thing that you need to make sure that you have for a wedding gown emergency is a needle and thread, and make sure the thread matches the color of the dress. Buttons and beads can come off, which is an easy fix. I recently heard a story of a wedding coordinator having to sew the bride into her wedding gown twenty minutes before the wedding!

Shifting from the bride to the groom, let's talk about what to do when his attire goes wrong. Well, let's be honest, will anyone even notice? Maybe we should shift our time preparing for other wedding emergencies.

Since your wedding day is a tapestry of a crazy amount of details, expect other things to go wrong. Here are a few cases that will help you think ahead and plan for a less stressful day.

Think about the color of your wedding cake icing. I had a friend use dark purple icing on her wedding cupcakes. While it was beautiful, she did not anticipate her groom smashing the cupcake in her face- all fun and games until the bride has a big purple stain on her face. So, if you want a dark color for your icing, either agree to not smash the cake in each others' face or have a few cupcakes in a different lighter color. Now keep in mind that sometimes a guy will promise not to smash it in your face, but then he gets caught up in the fun of the moment and does it anyway. Just saying.

Every bride can attest to the frustration of having guests confirm their reservation at the reception and not show up. On the flip side, most brides can also agree that guests who did not rsvp or even said that they were not coming, and show up are just as frustrating. An easy way to prepare for this fun surprise is to have a few extra chairs set throughout the reception hall. Chances are that some people who said that they were coming will not, which will balance out any of those surprise guests. However, if you prepare for the unexpected, then the worst that can happen is that you have extra seating.

One of my favorite wedding surprise stories is of a friend of mine who got married and had an inebriated family member decide to get up and sing a song for them at the reception. Luckily in her situation, the wedding singer ended up having a great voice and it only created a little tension. My advice? Let someone else deal with it. You wedding party should know the course of events for the day. If grandma gets up there to sing to you one of the groomsmen or even a parent of the bride or groom should easily, and without drawing too much attention, direct them to an exit to deal with the situation. The worst that can happen is they embarrass you for a few minutes and someone gets in on video so that you can revisit the moment on youtube after the wedding. Just remember that it will be funny, if not yet then later.

Children are adorable and for some reason it has become a tradition to put little boys in a cute tux and little girls in a small white dress to have them walk down the aisle. When you stop to think about it, how is it that we as adults expect a small child, who is inevitably unpredictable, to walk down the aisle with hundreds of people watching them? However, most brides want their little nephew, niece, or any other cute kid to be a part of their wedding. So here is the truth: a lot of kids, of any age, find that when faced with hundreds of people watching them all they want is their mom or dad; or, like the flower girl in my friend's wedding: to sit down in the middle of the aisle with her flower girl basket and scream at an unbelievable decibel. Kids are unpredictable, so sometimes the best thing to do is have the flower girl or ring bearer walk down the aisle with one of the bridesmaids that they are comfortable with, their mom, or even the bride. I saw a video of a ring bearer who got so scared walking down the aisle, that he ran up and hit the videographer. So, this is a basic fight or flight principle that you need to anticipate.

Another accident to anticipate that involves the ring bearer is his losing the rings. Again, with the ring bearer being a child it may not be the wisest decision to entrust such an important and expensive object with him. A wedding coordinator suggested that the fake rings be put on the ring pillow and give the actual rings to the best man. You don't want to be standing at the altar with no ring to give to your beloved.

These are just a few scenarios that can be anticipated and dealt with
before the big day. Like I said before, there are a lot of things that can
go wrong. With so many details and so many integrated parts that make
up this day, you have to leave a little room for at least a few mishaps.
And once you get to the big day keep in mind that the best thing you
as the bride can do is relax. You will be walking down the aisle toward
the person that you love, and a drunk relative or lack of napkins will not
change or even ruin that. So take a deep breath, relax, and enjoy one of
the most important and amazing days of your life.

CHAPTER 23

CARING FOR YOUR DRESS AFTER THE RECEPTION AND HOW TO PROPERLY PRESERVE YOUR GOWN AS A KEEPSAKE

JOY SALYARDS

You have spent many hours and put much thought in the selection of your wedding gown. Your hope is that someday your daughter will wear your gown on her special day. The gown was most likely the most expensive article of clothing you have ever purchased; even if it was not the most expensive it is the most valuable as far as sentiment is concerned. Your gown could be passed down from generation to generation or remade as a new gown for your future granddaughter or as a christening gown for your future great-granddaughter. But, no matter you will want to preserve your wedding gown as a remembrance of your special day and how you looked on your special day as you walked down the aisle. After you spent all the time, effort, and resources into finding your perfect gown, you must use the necessary procedures to preserve your perfect gown. Since, the gown itself holds so many memories and has so much sentimental history. Your gown is a treasured memento, and if cleaned and preserved properly will last for many years to come.

Your question is how do I preserve my wedding gown. Well, after the wedding most brides have the best of intentions as far as their gown is concerned. But soon days turn into weeks, and weeks into months, and then into years. This procrastination can cause serious damage to your gown. It is vital that your special gown be cleaned properly. Not all dry cleaners are equipped to clean a wedding gown. The gown should not smell like cleaning fluid when you pick it up from the cleaners. Fortunately there are many wedding gown preservation companies that specialize in the cleaning and preserving of wedding gowns. Ideally the gown should be preserved within days or weeks of the wedding to assure the best cleaning and preservation possible.

Gown preservation companies take all the necessary steps to pre-treat your gown for spots. The best method for dry cleaning a wedding gown is the use of virgin solvent. Virgin solvent is not only good for the environment but is also good for your wedding gown. Gowns cleaned in virgin solvent will not have a dry clean smell. There is no odor in the gown. Some gowns will require a wet-cleaning method also. Wet cleaning is the best for sugar stains, food stains and dirty hem lines. The wet cleaning method leaves no chemicals in the gown and also removes the sizing from your gown. Sizing is well liked by mice and other insects.

Professional gown cleaners and preservers use both methods depending on the fabric of the gown. Experience is an important factor when selecting a company to clean and preserve your special gown. Be sure to check with your local bridal salon to see whom they would recommend to clean and preserve your gown.

Here are some questions you may want to ask a dry cleaner if you are not using a cleaning and preservation service:

1. Does the dry cleaner do the work in-house or do they send the gown off premises?

2. Do they use dry-cleaning or wet-cleaning?

3. If the company would be dry-cleaning your gown, what type of solvent are they using?

4. How many years of experience does this dry-cleaner have with wedding gowns? Who is doing the cleaning and pressing of their gowns? How experienced is the person that is doing this task?

5. Is this cleaner using virgin solvent to clean the wedding gown?

You as the consumer need to know several things about your wedding gown:

1. What type of fabric is your gown made from?

2. What kind of cleaning does the care label on your gown suggest? If it states dry-clean only, does it also have a symbol for water cleaning? Please look very carefully; the label may say professional dry-cleaning or professional wet-cleaning recommended.

3. Hot dirty is your gown? What type of stains does it have (perspiration, wine, food, make-up, etc.)?

4. Is you gown beaded and sequined? Will they need special treatment? Are they sewed on or glued on?

If your gown and/or lining is silk, rayon, or acetate and does not have beads or sequins you should be able to have it cleaned by a dry-cleaner that uses perchloroethylene (perc). For gowns of these fabrics that is a plus, because perc is the best degreaser and this cleaning fluid works great on very dirty hemlines. If your gown is made of these fabrics and does have sequins and beads then the Stoddard formula, Hyrdo-carbon or Greenearth will be the best to use.

Make sure you point out any stains to your dry-cleaner. Also be sure to point out any spills on the gown, even if they do not show. Dry-cleaning fluids will not remove sugar stains, so the gown needs to be pre-treated. Professional gown cleaning and preservation companies automatically take your gown through all the necessary steps with out you telling them this information. This is what they do every day and in many cases have been doing for nearly 100 years.

If your gown and lining are polyester, having no beads and sequins or having beads and sequins, wet cleaning is the best method for your gown.

Professional gown preservation companies have common goals to protect your gown from:

- Yellowing

- Permanent creasing

- Mildew

- Mold

- Oxidation spots

- Light

- Dust

Yellowing occurs with age if not pre-treated. The plastic bag you store your wedding gown in can be a culprit that causes the yellowing of your gown. Most plastics give off fumes that promote yellowing. Even with proper care, some fabrics tend to yellow more than others and it may be impossible to prevent all yellowing.

Usually, silk fabrics have a tendency to yellow more than synthetic fabrics such as polyester, rayon and acetate. But nylon which is a synthetic fabric does have the tendency to yellow more than other synthetic fabrics. Gowns that are wet-cleaned have an advantage over solvent cleaned gowns when it comes to yellowing. Preserving your gown in an acid-free environment is your best protection against your gown yellowing.

Flat storage is recommended for garments when ever possible. However, because of the size of wedding gowns, it is impractical.

Keeping your gown in a breathable environment will protect it best from both mildew and mold growth. When fibers can breathe mold and mildew does not survive.

Oxidation spots occur when a substance has not been cleaned properly; the spot oxidizes and turns brown. This happens when the gown has not been cleaned properly and the dry-cleaning solvents did not remove all the substances on the gown. Spills from clear soda or wine may not be noticed at the time of the initial cleaning. Unless these spills are pre-treated, it is likely they will oxidize over time. The sooner an oxidized stain is caught, the more likely it will be able to be removed.

Keeping your gown covered will protect it from light and dust.

Remember that your gown holds so many memories and the picture of you and your gown will be around for over 100 years. Have your gown professionally cleaned and preserved to keep your memories in the best of shape.

CHAPTER 24

YOUR WEDDING DAY CHECKLIST

MARY MARR

I can just imagine your excitement and joy when you first received your engagement ring from the "man of your dreams". I'm sure that some of you were taken by surprise as you had no idea that your fiancé was going to propose to you so early in your relationship. And I'll bet that others felt that they had been waiting so long for this moment that they were beginning to wonder if it was ever going to come.

Those of you who waited a long time may have secretly planned your entire wedding before you even received your ring, while others who were taken by surprise, may not have had the clarity of mind to think about wedding plans until the initial surprise of the proposal was past.

One thing for sure, at some point all of you have come to the realization that your wedding celebration is really going to be take place and you'll want to start working on your plans for this as soon as possible.

After receiving your ring, you had to decide how you were going to announce your engagement to others. Someone may have hosted an engagement party for your family and close friends or you may have decided to mail an engagement announcement to them. Some couples prefer to put their engagement picture and announcement in their local paper so that everyone gets the chance to read it at the same time. If this is what you are planning to do, when announcing the details of your upcoming wedding, it is best to generalize your wedding date rather than give out specific information to people you don't know. Unfortunately, some brides and grooms who announced the exact date of their wedding, later reported home invasions that took place while they were gone away on their honeymoon. We can only try to imagine the terrible disappointment they felt upon returning home.

– At least 12 months in advance

Most engagement periods are approximately 9 – 14 months long, so unless you are planning on having a longer engagement period, you need to start making wedding plans now. The very first thing that you will need to do is to have a very good idea of what you can AFFORD! If family members have offered to help with the expenses of your wedding, you should have a private conversation with each of them as early as possible so that you are aware of what they are planning to contribute. You will not be able to go forward with your wedding budget until this is done.

There are many wedding planning sites on the internet from which you can print out a wedding budget. They are wonderful guides in helping couples sort out their wedding finances in a very systematic way. They cover most of the general expense categories to get you started. Remember, the percentages suggested for each expense category are not set in stone, so you will have the flexibility that you require to spend a little more here and a little less there, as long as you stay on track with your total expenditures. Having a well-thought out realistic wedding budget is as important to you as having a map or GPS when you travel away from home. A good map can help you navigate safely just as a well-planned wedding budget can guide you joyfully to your wedding day.

Besides your wedding budget, you will want to purchase a good Day-Timer that allows you to keep track of appointments and events. You will also want a record keeping system for payments and contracts, and a binder to hold pictures of venue options, your bridal gown, your maids' outfits, fabric swatches, color samples, and everything else that you will want to keep handy during the planning stage. If possible, try to find an all-in-one system that isn't too cumbersome to be portable.

Deciding on a Wedding Planner

One of the first things that you may want to consider once you know what your finances are is whether you will want or need to hire a wedding planner. Professional wedding planners who are experienced in planning weddings in your area and within your culture can be worth their weight in gold. I would suggest that one of the deciding questions that you may want to ask yourself is, "Do you realistically have the time it will take to plan your own wedding?" If you have the luxury of time, some creative genius, some organizational skills, and you enjoy making decisions, then you likely don't need the help of a wedding planner. However, if the very thought of planning a wedding makes you sick and keeps you up at night, you may want to check out what a wedding planner has to offer you.

You can hire a wedding planner to take care of every detail of your wedding for you. In that case, his/her fee will be approximately 10% of your wedding budget. If you don't need or want this much help, you can hire a wedding planner to only assist you with the help that you need. Although the expense of hiring a wedding planner may seem daunting, an experienced wedding planner with an excellent reputation should have so much experience from planning all kinds of events that he/she will likely have all kinds of cost effective ideas to offer you. It is possible that the expense of hiring a professional could be offset by the efficiency of services rendered.

Your Ceremony – 12 months

Budget Allowance – 3%

No matter if you are planning your own wedding or a wedding planner is doing it for you, one of the first things that you will want to consider is where your wedding ceremony will take place. Will it be at a church, in a garden, at a resort, or at your reception venue? Regardless of where it is, you will want to remember that the purpose of inviting guests to your ceremony is so that they can be witnesses to the vows that you and your fiancé are making that day. Your vows should be of such importance to you that you will want to be able to create a serene, thoughtful atmosphere in which you deliver them. That's not to say that your ceremony shouldn't be filled with joy and laughter. You and your fiancé and your officient will want to plan a wedding ceremony that includes both joy and solemnity and which has real meaning to you and your guests.

Be sure to include in your ceremony expenses the ceremony location fee, your officient's fee, the cost of your marriage license, musician's fees, etc. Include everything that you will require to give your ceremony site the ambience that you are looking for.

This is a good time to bring up pre-marital counseling. If you are given an opportunity to participate in pre-marital classes, you would be wise to look into what they have to offer. Divorce statistics today tell us that 50% of all first marriages fail, yet no one plans a wedding celebration believing that they will be divorcing at some point in the future. All of us think that we are going to be the ones that beat the odds, yet only half of us manage to do so. The benefit of taking pre-marital classes is that you will have a qualified professional opinion help you sort out any tangles that already exist in your relationship. In some cases, you won't even know that they already exist, yet a trained counselor can see the red flags already there. When a counselor is able to reveal these to you, you will have an opportunity to see a successful history of change take place before the wedding day. When these potential marriage destroyers are put to rest so early in the relationship, you will have a much greater chance of beating the odds. Can you imagine the difference this can make for your life? Even if you have to pay for this service, you would be wise to invest in your marriage before investing in other budget items that aren't nearly as critical.

Your Reception – 12 months

Budget allowance 48%
After deciding where your ceremony will take place, you will want to consider where your wedding reception will take place. This is the single most expensive part of your wedding planning, as it generally consumes approximately 48 – 50% of your entire wedding budget. To get started you will need to create an approximate guest list. Once you know how many guests you are planning to invite to your wedding reception, you will be able to decide how much money you can afford to allot per person/per plate. Once you have calculated this dollar figure, you can begin to look for a venue that fills your needs. Depending on your budget, you may need to get creative with your reception planning. For example, if you can't afford an eight course dinner at the Taj Mahal, how about a candle lit wine and cheese event later in the evening. Another idea to consider may be a buffet lunch following a morning ceremony. Or you may decide to have your wedding ceremony and reception on a week day rather than on the weekend. There are so many ways that you can tweak your plans to have an affordable, yet fabulous wedding day. The earlier you start planning, the more time you have to let your creative genius flow.

Whatever your ceremony and reception plans include, remember to be considerate of your guests at all times. You are inviting them to celebrate with you on the most important day of your life, and your goal should be to look after them, so that they will know that their presence was appreciated by you. You may not be aware of the fact that it is not considered poor etiquette for your invited guests to attend without bringing you a wedding gift. Although it is generally our custom to bring a gift to a wedding, some of your guests may choose not to. Therefore, when planning your wedding budget it is wise to plan around the money you have before your wedding, rather than count on the money you think you might have after your wedding. It is not necessary to go into debt to have an extraordinary wedding day celebration.

Your reception costs should include your guests' food and drink, your rentals such as chairs, tables, table cloths and napkins, favours, and the cost of your cake. When choosing your venue, remember to ask the establishment's event coordinator what is included in the cost per plate price? For example, does it include chair covers, table covers, napkins, centerpieces, the wedding cake, and so on? You will find there can be quite a difference from one place to another. A lovely venue that includes these items in its price may be more affordable in the long run than a less attractive venue, where you will need to incur all kinds of additional costs in creating the ambience that you want. Once again it will be very important to make sure that you understand all of the facts before signing a contract that will disappoint you in the future.

Your Honeymoon - 12 months

Budget Allowance – 3%
Some wedding budget planners will not include this category as a part of your wedding expense, as it is not directly related to your wedding day. However, since you'll need to set aside the finances ahead of time, it is a good idea to factor this in now. I believe very strongly in the value of a honeymoon, and I would encourage you to plan on having one, even if it means that you need to spend less money on something else.

There is no more wonderful way to begin your married life together than to go away together all alone. Throughout the months of wedding planning, with so many details to take care of and so many people to depend on, it is very possible that you will be feeling some negative stress from time to time. You will have a much better chance of keeping "your eyes on the light at the end of the tunnel," if you know that you have a honeymoon to look forward to as soon as the wedding celebration is over.

The value of a honeymoon is not related to the money spent for it. Therefore, there is no need to plan a trip that you can't afford. Whether someone gifts you with a week at their cottage or you plan a Mediterranean cruise, the whole point of a honeymoon is to allow the two of you to be able to reflect on the wonder of your wedding day and the amazing commitment that you have made to each other. So quickly, when the honeymoon is over, you will have to get back to the real world where there may not be time to do this again. But the memory of a wonderful, meaningful honeymoon that the two of you shared together can carry you over a million obstacles down the road.

Your Wedding Attire – 12 months

Budget Allowance 10%

Once you have given thought to your wedding venue, the time of year that you will be celebrating your wedding, and the degree of formality that you are going for, you are ready to go out and shop for your gown. There is generally nothing more important to the bride on her wedding day than the way that she wishes to present herself to her groom, as she glides gracefully down the aisle to meet him.

The best advice that I can give you is for you to book yourself an appointment at one of the most reputable full service bridal salons in your area. Make sure that you pick a place that is known to keep up with the trends. In most cases, a bridal salon that requires appointments will be the place to go for that one-on-one service that you deserve and will learn to love. Knowing ahead of time that a professional sales consultant is waiting to meet you when you arrive should help you to relax and encourage you to be yourself when you go.

Be prepared to share your wedding plans with your consultant by showing her any pictures that you may already have, which will help her catch your vision of what your wedding is all about. Once your bridal consultant has had a chance to hear you, she will likely contribute some ideas of her own that she can add to yours, to help make your wedding day a magical one. Be prepared to share your budget with her soon after meeting her. You will be very pleased to find that a professional bridal consultant will count it a privilege to serve you no matter what price point you want to meet.

When you begin to try on gowns, it will not be unusual for your consultant to suggest a few styles that you may not have considered before. Remember, this is her field of expertise, and she has been trained and is experienced in what styles may look best on you. Furthermore, she'll also be aware of the latest trends coming forward in the bridal fashion industry. You can rely on her to use every resource available to her to help you find the "gown of your dreams".

The benefit of choosing a full service bridal salon from the start is that it also specializes in maids' gowns, mothers' dresses, flower girls' attire, and accessories. When all items have been carefully and thoughtfully chosen to enhance and compliment each other, you will have a total designer look presentation of yourself, your mom, and your maids.

This 10% budget expenditure is to be allotted for all of your personal expenses related to your wedding day which include your gown, all of your accessories, and your aesthetic services on that day. If you do go over your budget when choosing your bridal gown, there will be lots of categories that you can cut back on so that you can afford your "once-in-a-life time dream wedding gown".

Your Attendants – 11 months
In general, both male and female attendants cover the costs of their own clothes, accessories, and aesthetics for your wedding day. If you haven't already made decisions regarding your wedding attendants, you will want to do that as soon as you can. Choose from your closest friends and family members. Choose those you know are dependable and will appreciate the honour that you are bestowing on them.

That being said, it is important for you to recognize that you are asking them to make a rather sizable investment of both time and money in standing up for you that day. If you are aware that some of the folks that you would like to invite may have financial and time restraints in fulfilling their duties, it is best for you to have a private talk with them beforehand. If you find out that money and/or time will be a problem, you can invite your friends to fill a different position that won't be as demanding, such as monitoring the guest book or seating plan. If you choose to invite someone in need into your wedding party anyway, you should graciously assist him/her with their financial obligations and/or relieve them of as many duties that you can. By doing this you will eliminate any negative feelings that could arise down the road.

Before actually shopping with your attendants for their attire, you should take the time to figure out how you would like them to present themselves on your wedding day. It is generally not a good idea for a bride to tell her maids that they can wear whatever they want, because most brides in the end won't really mean it. Before going out shopping as a group, it would be a good idea for you to make another personal appointment at your bridal salon. Your personal consultant already knows the vision that you have for your wedding day and she will be pleased to help you carry this through in the choices that are made for your maids dresses too.

The Groom's Attire - 3 months

Budget Allowance 2%
Depending on the formality of your gown, your groom will want to choose his attire and that of his attendants to compliment your gown and your bridesmaids' gowns. If you are having a casual event, the groom and his party may wish to appear in linen pants with linen blend shirts and fabulous ties, rather than donning the more traditional tuxedo look. The important thing that will be sure to give you that "million dollar" look is that thought and careful planning go into coordinating it all.

If there is any fear about what your groomsmen may decide to wear to your wedding, it might be better to remove all options, rather than leave this to chance. In that case, it may be best to have all of the guys rent tuxedos, including socks, shoes, shirts, and ties. That way, there won't be any last minute not-so-pleasant surprises to deal with on your wedding day.

If renting tuxedos, it is far more efficient to deal with a shop that has its own tuxedo inventory and does alterations right on site. That way any tailoring issues that may arise prior to your wedding day can be easily corrected.

Wedding Rings –6 months

Budget Allowance 3%
This expenditure does include the wedding bands, but does not include the engagement ring, as it is assumed that the engagement ring was already paid for before it was presented to the bride.

Your wedding bands play a very significant part on your wedding day and are usually exchanged during your wedding ceremony. Their circular shape is symbolic of your love for each other, which has no end. Your wedding rings are worthy of you putting some thought and energy into choosing them. Instead of just visiting your local big box jewelry department or your jewelry chain store, why not visit a custom jeweler that makes custom wedding bands on site? A professional goldsmith/ gemologist has the ability to create anything that you can imagine, and because he would have all the gems and metals on site, he could advise you as to how you can tweak your ideas to keep your budget on track. Customizing your wedding rings could make a significant, delightful difference to both of you, bringing you immense pleasure and a renewed sense of marital intimacy every time you wear them.

Flowers – 9 months

Budget Allowance 7%

Flowers are a long standing welcome feature that you will find at every special event. That is because there is nothing that can lend its fragrance and beauty to a room in quite the same way, whether it is a single rose freshly cut from the garden, or a professionally designed bouquet. For your wedding day, when you plan for flowers, think of your bouquet, your attendants' bouquets, corsages, boutonnieres, and centerpieces.

The best thing for you to do is to make an appointment with your local reputable florist. Make sure that you pick a florist with a history of business longevity on their side, yet who demonstrates flair and knowledge of current floral design trends. Business longevity means the florist likely has experienced every kind of problem at some point in his/her career and has a back-up plan to handle them all. However, just having longevity without style likely won't give you the look that you are going for. A florist who stocks lots of different kinds of flowers would be one of the best choices for you to counsel with, if you, like most of us, do not have a great familiarity with the names of flowers. That way, the florist can show you first hand how the colours come together for the look that you want. If you openly share your budget with your florist at the beginning of your consultation time, he/she will be able to show you how to change the cost of your bouquets simply by tweaking the flowers, fillers, and design elements, and yet still give you the designer look that you want.

Music – 12 months

Budget Allowance 7%

Nothing will influence the mood of your event in the same way that music can. One way to cut expenses without sacrificing class would be for you to hire a talented pianist, who can play completely different genres of music at both your ceremony and cocktail hour. Be sure to ask friends and relatives, whose opinions you trust, for referrals, but make sure you have the artists personally play or sing for you before you contract with them. Keep in mind that no matter how delicious the meal was, or how delighted your guests were before the dance began, a bad band or DJ can spoil the rest of the night and have your crowd leaving for home sooner than you'd like. Choosing quality music performers, within your budget, will be money well spent.

Photography – 12 months

Budget Allowance 10%

They say a picture is worth a thousand words, and at no time is this truer than when you get the amazing privilege of viewing a spectacular shot. When it comes to your wedding photos, it is best for you to hire the services of an artist who has ample wedding experience under their belt. That way if anything unsuspected happens your photographer will know exactly what to do about it and your "once in a lifetime" wedding photo opportunities won't be lost forever. If you watch today's photographers on a photo shoot, it may seem to you that all they do is shoot, shoot, shoot, a million digital shots without applying any technical savvy at all. Everything seems to happen so fast that you may have the impression that anyone with a camera in hand can take pictures with the same result. However, that just isn't true. You still need to think about hiring a professional photographer/videographer to get the most out of your wedding day. When interviewing a photographer you'll want to make an appointment to go to his/her studio to see samples of what can be achieved. Be sure to ask a lot of questions while you are there. Inquire about your photographer's goals for your wedding day to ensure that they line up with yours in a way that makes you completely comfortable. If you feel even slightly intimidated, your tension may show up in every shot. Choose a professional that you feel good about, and only contract for the services that you can afford.

Above all, remember to plan long in advance, so that you can get your "beauty sleep" the week of your wedding, so that you'll be camera ready on your special day.

Transportation – 10 months

Budget Allowance 2%

How will you travel to your ceremony site, to your photo shoot site, to your reception site, and to your wedding night accomodations? These are all questions that you need to answer long before your wedding day. If you have a large wedding party and large families, who are participating in photo shoots, you will really need to think in terms of getting everyone where they need to be on time. Any delays in the schedule can make a problem when it comes to getting to your reception on time. You don't want your guests feeling half-starved, waiting past the dinner hour for you to arrive.

The options for you to choose from are endless. They run all the way from horse and buggy to Hummer limousines. When making your travel decisions, the most important thing to take into consideration is the reliability of the people involved. Can you trust your wedding party to follow a map or GPS and practice drive the route before your wedding day? Is there anyone who will commit to enforcing the schedule, so everyone is where they need to be on time? If you have confidence that everyone will stay on track, then planning for transportation is not as critical a job. However, if any red flags go off for you just thinking about this, you may be better off hiring a limousine or a limo bus, depending on the numbers of people involved.

Once again, be sure that you don't just go for the cheapest price. You want to pick a transportation expert based on professionalism and reliability. A good limo company will want all of your particulars far in advance of your wedding day, as their driver/drivers will take it upon themselves to make sure that they have everyone where they need to be on time. If you have to tweak your wedding budget to make this happen, it will be worth it to you, just to have the confidence you need to be at peace on your wedding day.

Stationery- 9 months

Budget Allowance 3%
This category expense should cover wedding invitations, response cards, thank you notes, postage, guest book, seating plan, and so on. One way that you can purchase wedding invitations is by shopping with a company that offers cookie-cutter invitations with preset designs. You can order these invites with your name and wedding date on them. This was the traditional way of doing things for the past 50 years.

However, now that weddings have become extremely personalized, you have many more options. I would like to suggest that you take the time to consider one of the most awesome choices available to you. Why not book an appointment with a stationery artist first? These creative geniuses can help you customize your wedding invitations to reflect you and your wedding theme. And the best part of all is that this privilege may not cost you any more than it would to place an order from a book. I have visited with one such artist and have seen for myself the wonder of what can be done.

If you plan to make your wedding stationery yourself, you may still want to pay for a consultation with a custom designer before getting started. Be sure to be honest with the artist about the reason for your appointment when you book the meeting so that you won't get caught in an embarrassing moment.

Gifts –6 months

Budget Allowance 2%
In this category, your budgeted amount needs to cover gifts for your bridesmaids, groomsmen, your parents, and any other special people that you want to honour on your day. Just take the total number of gifts that you want to purchase and divide your total budget for this category by this number to get the average price per gift that you can afford. Again, you may need to get very creative with this category.

If you think ahead of all the possible gifts you may want to buy, every time you go shopping, you will have this information in the back of your mind. That way, if you spot a certain item that suits your budget, you can make your purchase right away.

Another idea that you may want to investigate is the concept of shopping for gifts at the businesses with whom you are already dealing. For example, your bridal shop may offer you special prices on jewelry for you to purchase for your maids to wear on your wedding day.

When purchasing gifts for special people, try to find something special just for them, so that they will know how much you appreciate their involvement.

Final Thoughts

It takes a lot of time and energy to plan a wedding! There will be many opportunities for you to become side-tracked, and forget what this day is all about. If you and your fiancé lose your focus you shouldn't be surprised when everyone else does too. It is up to you to remember that your entire celebration is about the love that the two of you have for each other and about the commitment that you are making that day. Going into debt to have a wedding isn't necessary at all. Hosting a late afternoon cocktail party on your wedding day can be just as celebratory as a full blown black tie event. In fact, a wedding ceremony scheduled on a Sunday, immediately following the regular church service, and then enhanced with a luncheon afterwards, can be beautiful, too.

Planning your wedding should not be giving you nightmares at night. Keep cool, keep focused, and remember what this event is all about. In so doing, when things don't always turn out as planned, you won't lose your mind over them. Remember that no one and nothing can steal your joy, unless you allow them.

Happy planning! May you have the most joy-filled, fabulous wedding day of all. And more importantly, may your love for each other grow deeper and richer with every year!